I0024116

Lucy Helen Yates

The Profession of Cookery, from a French point of View

with some Economical practices peculiar to the Nation

Lucy Helen Yates

The Profession of Cookery, from a French point of View
with some Economical practices peculiar to the Nation

ISBN/EAN: 9783744789660

Printed in Europe, USA, Canada, Australia, Japan

Cover: Foto ©Andreas Hilbeck / pixelio.de

More available books at **www.hansebooks.com**

THE

PROFESSION OF COOKERY

from a French point of view.

WITH SOME ECONOMICAL PRACTICES PECULIAR TO THE NATION.

BY

LUCY H. YATES,

LECTURER TO THE INTERNATIONAL HORTICULTURAL EXHIBITION
COMMITTEE.

WARD, LOCK & BOWDEN, LIMITED,

LONDON: WARWICK HOUSE, SALISBURY SQUARE, E.C

NEW YORK AND MELBOURNE.

1894

[All rights reserved.]

CONTENTS.

THE PROFESSION OF COOKERY.

INTRODUCTORY.

COOKERY has long been thought to be an art, and one also for which a special gift is required, if any great degree of perfection therein is to be attained.

This is perfectly true, and a thoroughly good cook will be no mean "artist" in every sense of the word.

But very few people, even among those who are daily employed in cooking, will give the same amount of patience and diligence to attain the distinction of meriting the term "artist" in this most important of professions as they would give to gain a knowledge of music or painting, or to learn a language.

And yet the preparation and serving of the food we eat, in a right or a wrong manner, is the very foundation of our home life; not only does the health of the inmates greatly depend upon the cook, but their tempers and spirits also.

It is just in this part of the household where what are commonly called " brains " tell to most advantage, and where, alas, they are most seldom thought to be needed.

Upon method, skill, and economy in the kitchen depend so much the well-being of the household, and these can rarely be found where the kitchen is under the rule of a kitchen maid, or even of the modern " good plain cook."

This department is as well worthy of the best considerations of every true *lady* as any of the many " higher branches " which claim her atten- tion in the world to-day.

The training—even the classical training— which she receives at school need never unfit, but rather make her the more apt a pupil when she gives the same amount of attention to learn this profession which she gave to mathematics.

Brains tell everywhere, *particularly* in the

kitchen. If our girls and young women would study cookery as they study French and German, starting from the A, B, C, and progressing upwards, step by step, studying it in all its branches until they might be said to have "graduated," there would then be hope that our kitchens might become as attractive to visit as the studio or the music room.

The knowledge of how to save labour, and economise not only time, but strength—which is the real test of the practical from the theoretical—in this profession as in all others, is only acquired by the earnest student.

If the natural taste for this be dull, the more need to lay to it strength of will—resolution born of a just judgment of the importance of the knowledge she would acquire.

On the other hand, however good her intentions may be, without this knowledge a great deal of toil will be needlessly expended; the result mortification, and the heavy, wearing sense of inferiority that puts the novice so soon out of heart.

In treating cookery as a profession there will be found ample scope for various degrees of talent; all who enter for it should be willing to pay the premium and give the necessary time to learn it thoroughly. As the very lowliest occupation is dignified by the manner in which it is performed, so nothing is " menial " or beneath the attention of her who would excel or assist others to excel in this department of the world's work, essentially the woman's province, where she reigns and rules by right of special fitness.

THE PROFESSION OF COOKERY.

CHAPTER I.

Economy as the Soul of Cookery.

TRUE economy is the soul of good cookery. There is, perhaps, no word so little understood as this word economy. It is too often considered to mean parsimony, meanness, or stinginess. It will invariably be found the better the cook the more economy will be practised.

What a so-called "good plain cook" will throw away or consign to the dog-kennel, an ingenious French artiste will make into an entrée or an entremet of the most tempting kind.

The French are a nation of cooks, and they cannot afford to dine without soup; yet in England, the most frequent excuse given for

P.C.   B

the absence of the soup is the cost as well as the trouble of preparing it.

Sometimes it is urged that "We think soup disagrees with us," or "My husband can't take soup": and yet no Frenchman, whatever his status in life, would think his meal complete without his "potage." Is there any reason to suppose his digestive organs are constructed on a different plan to his brother Englishman's?

The real reason—when soup is found to disagree—may generally be traced to its overstrength. It is not intended to furnish solid nutriment, but to supply a want felt by most people for something warm and savoury to begin the meal with, and it will also be found to greatly lessen the thirst for drink afterwards, hence effecting a saving in the wine cupboard.

Among the poor, a simple nourishing vegetable soup would be found of great value, largely dispensing with the, at present, almost inevitable jug of beer, to which recourse is had so frequently to "wash down" or make up for a dinner often far from appetising.

The saving, also, in the consumption of meat when soup takes the precedence, is no small argument in its favour.

Take, for example, the ordinary mid-day meal of the French " ouvrier." The soup pot has been put on the stove at an early hour; it contains carrots, turnips, potatoes, peas, haricots, leeks, etc., with a " bouquet " (a variety of herbs) and sorrel in abundance; the only thing of the nature of meat is a small piece of salted pork, and this, with plenty of water, is left to boil gently until required, often for several hours.

The pork is almost dissolved by this time; if not, it is cut very small, and returned to the pot, the contents of which go through the " passoir," or colander. It is well seasoned, and is then ready to pour into plates; substantial, satisfying, and with a mighty hunch of bread, this forms the staple of his meal. If he be well off, a piece of meat and a salad may follow this; but among the poor, a little fruit is thought quite sufficient.

On Sundays, high days, and festivals, he will partake of " bouillon "—a small piece of beef from the leg, boiled with the vegetables, but left clear this time, and the vegetables served on a separate dish—the meat served afterwards.

Of course, in different parts of the country

this simple menu may vary somewhat, but in southern France, where, if anywhere, economy is to be found in perfection, it rarely consists of anything more.

Among the peasants of the Vosges mountains it is still more simple, their diet, year in, year out, being mainly made up of potatoes, onions, and bread ; yet they are a hardy a sinewy race.

The Swiss peasantry also greatly resemble their French neighbours in their diet, with the exception that they eat rather more meat—the colder climate naturally calls for it ; but true thrift, economy in small things, is characteristic of both nations.

All nations may learn from one another ; as a rule, English people have much to learn in the art of thrifty cookery. They have not the faculty possessed by their neighbours across the silver streak, of making a delightful some-thing out of the despised remains, too often, alas ! cast away as worthless.

The thrifty bourgeoise, trotting along in the early morning with her market basket, would be horrified to see the English butchers' shops with their piles of stale scraps and trimmings all thrown to one side, ·just beginning to go bad, and sending out an odour which makes the butcher's stall a trial to visit; the fat portions and suet all mixed up together, while the prime joints are being lavishly cut off.

One of the great French "chefs" has said that English meat could not be surpassed; when good, it needed no sauce with it, being of a richer quality itself. That is true, but only when one can purchase of the best.

Take a butcher's shop in a provincial French town : your first thought on entering would be "how very little there is to buy," and you see all there is too—each piece set out on a separate hook, the well scrubbed tables and counters; while as to fat (!) there is scarcely a morsel to be had.

Every part of the different animals has its own special destiny to fulfil, no portion is of greater honour than another. Madame's eye is ever on the watch for the morsels for her "ragout," and the "marchand de frites" has been beforehand with them all, collecting the suet for his frying-pan.

Then, again, amongst the vegetables : English vegetables are not inferior in quality, yet they lack the freshness and the crispness—also the cleanliness—which makes this part of the market so attractive to visit in French towns :

neither is the supply anything like what it ought to be. Perhaps the " Small Holdings Act " may cause a change for the better in this respect.

In the present day, when the prices of provisions have so much increased, and still show an upward tendency, it is very needful for every family throughout the country to do all in their power to lessen the consumption of meat, thereby rendering it cheaper to those possessed of less wealth than themselves. It is a great mistake to depend too much upon meat.

Where bones are thrown away, and fresh meat is bought for soup making, it is certain that much nutritive matter is absolutely wasted, which under better management might be turned to good account.

Of the many delicious and even charming dishes composed of vegetables, few, indeed, are much known in English households ; yet their medicinal value is great, while they satisfy the appetite, and save the pocket at the same time.

A dainty "plat de légumes," served either before or with the joint of meat, thereby acting as a damper to the appetite, would be found to be true economy, especially in houses where

healthy children call to be fed. The variety—
ever capable of being extended—of these dishes
call for chapters to themselves.

With regard to economy in cookery, it will
have been seen, therefore, that it consists not
so much in living plainly, but rather in so
managing and arranging the various dishes
which compose the meal, that one shall spare
the other—by the use of simple means, lessen-
ing the consumption of the more expensive dish
or joint.

For the average housekeeper to do this easily
and effectively, she must bear in mind at least
two points: first, to keep herself *au courant* of
the commodities which are in season; the time
when any article in the market is most plentiful
and cheap will generally be found to be the
time when it is most wholesome for food.

"Early" or forced varieties are rarely desirable for ordinary food, however tempting
they may appear, and they are but seldom
bought by the truly thrifty housekeeper.

Throughout the winter months higher prices
are demanded for several kinds of food, but
the prudent and wise will "forestall the
market" in this respect, and lay in their stock
while they are at the cheapest.

There are ways and means of storing most vegetables and fruits, even in households where keeping room is limited; the main principle to be observed in storing perishable articles, is to exclude the air from them.

Another point to bear in mind, is to have the right quantity only, so far as can be judged, when providing for any particular dish. It is the " bits left over" which run away with the money.

In the South it is sometimes laughable to see how, when there happens to be a small portion left over, what skill is displayed in so turning it to account that it reappears under a fresh disguise, and forms a sensible addition to the next repast; but, as a rule, it takes the patience and skill of a genuine Frenchwoman to accomplish this feat.

One great reason of the economy of French methods of cooking is to be found in the utensils employed by them, and not a little is due to the different stoves. Of the latter there is a great variety.

The " bourgeoise Parisienne" has her charcoal stove, with its white tiles and the miniature baker's oven built in the wall; her roaster is quite a separate affair, resembling what is known in England as a "Dutch oven," but for all her only fuel is "wood coal"—"charbon de bois."

By the way, these charcoal stoves are so easy to set up, and so useful for many purposes, that it is a marvel they are so little known in England.

Built of brick, either in a recess or close to a kitchen wall; for neatness, the front and sides are covered with tiles, and the edges bound with iron. An opening a few inches square, with a grating above it, holds the charcoal, which lights rapidly and gives no smoke.

When not in use, the grating can be covered with a loose tile, and the flat top will serve as an extra table. During the course of a dinner it will render astonishing service for sauces, side dishes, etc.

In most French kitchens one of these furnaces is to be found, generally fitted with two or three gratings, and the "bourgeoise" will prefer to use it for her soup pot, rather than trust the latter to the more variable heat of her "cuisinière."

The true French cuisinière, or range, is very different, and in many respects much superior to, as well as far simpler than, its English compeer.

With its brightly polished table-like top and light ornamentation, it is an ornament to any room, and the consumption of fuel is so little— the heat being made to reach each part before it passes up the chimney—that it is wonderful such a clever inventive race as the English have yet so much to learn in the art of stove building.

To see their ranges, so heavily clamped and barred, one might think the food cooking therein was expected to take to itself wings and fly away.

Doubtless the labour attendant upon using these ranges is one reason why cooking is found to be such heavy work in middle-class households.

Nearly all French cooking vessels are made either of glazed earthenware or enamelled iron. In great houses the housekeeper will proudly show her extensive " batterie de cuisine " of immaculately shining copper; but these would be seldom used.

Nothing is found to surpass the "terrine" or earthen cooking vessels; they are long in reaching the boiling point, but they will retain the heat, and keep a more equable temperature longer than any other kind; and this slow cooking is an essential in most of their methods of cookery, particularly in soup making.

The favourite form for the " pot-au-feu " is a very deep one with a flat bottom, not very wide, and the sides sloping upwards to a slightly narrower opening at the top with a well-fitting lid. This makes the perfection of bouillon.

Where more rapid cooking is desirable, as in boiling of vegetables or sauces, nothing is found to equal enamelled iron, not easily burnt at the bottom, and quite easy to keep clean if only the cook will take the precaution of filling up the vessel with water immediately it is done with.

As the enamel retains the heat longer than plain iron, whatever remains on the surface hardens very quickly, making it a difficult matter to get off again once it is allowed to become dry. Where the enamel has become discoloured or stained, it may be made white again by boiling a little quicklime in the water.

Sand and powdered pumice-stone are excellent aids in cleaning saucepans, also earthenware vessels of all kinds.

A French housewife has her regular cleaning day for all her kitchen utensils, which is as faithfully observed as her washing day. Every article which admits of being polished is taken

down and literally *scrubbed* with sand and strong
soda water till it shines again; a final rinse in
hot water, and a wipe with a clean towel before
it is restored to its place.

All tinware, iron, copper, or brass utensils
are kept in excellent condition by this means;
one or two hours' steady labour will suffice.

French country people throughout the land,
and even the townspeople in the southern towns,
reckon to keep at least one pig; and this most
useful animal is turned to good account.

If he is not "the gintleman that pays the
rint," he at least does a very large share towards maintaining the family.

Killed in the autumn, by pickling, drying,
and various other methods of curing, his flesh
provides meat for all the winter at least, and
has the advantage of being always at hand
should an emergency arise in the shape of an
unexpected visitor.

There are professional pig slayers and curers,
whose sole business it is to do everything that
is required in regard to the animal. They make
the strings of sausages ready for smoking, the
hams for curing, the "black puddings," the
"pâtés," the "fromages de porc"; prepare
the pieces for the pickling tub, and, in fact,

undertake all the trouble and responsibility connected with the occasion.

Then is the grand opportunity of the year for the good "ménagère" to show her kind heart.

There is the generous portion for the "curé" or the "pasteur," according as her faith dictates ; the gift to be bestowed on a less fortunate friend or neighbour; and "the poor man at the gate" will not be overlooked.

With her pig safely disposed of, another growing up in the pen, her vegetables well stored and housed, her fruits preserved, and her "dame Jeanne" of oil in the cellar, the "bonne bourgeoise" is proof against invasion, in whatever form it may come.

In this simple, homely fashion of living, an unexpected guest is ever a welcome addition to the family table.

CHAPTER II.

Soups and Purées.

IN starting on the subject of soups in general, it will be well to classify them under three divisions: Clear, thickened, and "purées," or vegetable soups.

The distinction between thickened soup and a purée, lies in the fact of the former owing its consistency to the introduction of some artificial substance, such as rice, tapioca, flour, etc., while the purée is made by carefully pressing all the ingredients through a "tamis," or wire sieve.

Pea soup is really purée of peas, tomato soup purée of tomatoes, etc.

When rice, vermicelli, or macaroni are added to a clear soup or stock, they should have been previously boiled in water, otherwise they will be apt to give a cloudy appearance to the soup.

Clear soup may be simply "bouillon," or broth, from beef, mutton, or veal, or it may be

14

stock made from bones, or, again, the stock from shin of beef or veal.

The same principle of cooking applies to each and all—to bring it very slowly to boiling point, and never to let it boil hard.

Many French cooks put the meat intended for bouillon on the stove in nearly cold water, even when it is intended to be eaten afterwards; but where it is deemed preferable to keep a little more flavour in the meat, it should wait until the water nearly boils, then be plunged into the pot, and quickly come to boiling point again, after which it should be drawn aside from the fire, the vegetables added (either whole or merely split in two), the little bunch of herbs securely tied, then allowed to boil very gently for two or three hours.

It is not customary to serve any vegetables in the tureen with true French bouillon—they are placed on a dish, and handed round, or reserved to be eaten with the meat.

When making a broth from veal, it may be treated in the same way, only as veal takes a less time to cook, and soon becomes soft, it is better to remove it when sufficiently done, and make a different dish altogether of the meat.

When using *shin* of beef or veal, it would be

wasteful to treat it as the other parts of boiling meat, as it contains really more nutritious matter, which takes a much longer time to be extracted. It should be placed in a deep brown jar, and be relegated to the far corner of the oven, and left to cook for several hours; then carefully pour away all the liquor from it into a clean vessel, and put in a cold place.

When vegetables are required to be added to this, they should be boiled apart, never in this stock, which merely requires warming up as it is needed.

The meat, if carefully separated from all skin and gristle, liberally seasoned, and pounded in a mortar, makes very presentable potted meat, quite good enough for every-day family use.

Clear soup is also made from bones, cooked or uncooked, odds and ends of meat, and the carcases of poultry. Always bear in mind that it is *stock*, and to be treated as such.

No scraps or bones need ever be wasted. Chop all bones with a hatchet into very small pieces. All dry corners and trimmings of meat are valuable also, particularly if they are *brown*.

In soup made of this stock, vegetables may be added in a variety of ways. Cut very small indeed, and frizzled in a little clear fat till they are just brown, then it is known as "Julienne soup"; or cut small, and plain boiled, then it is "consommé" (either with or without the addition of rice and a little brown gravy); or the carrots may be grated, the remaining vegetables cut into dice.

It is to this kind of stock, also, that macaroni and vermicelli are added, and the same stock forms the foundation of mulligatawny and the richer kinds of soup, which properly come under the division of thickened soups.

If a thickened soup is still required *clear*, it may be kept so by using tapioca or potato-flour as the thickening medium.

If tapioca be added early enough, it will completely dissolve and become perfectly smooth; sago is a similar agent, but it never quite loses its grain, neither is it quite so clear. If ever ordinary flour be used, it will be found a great improvement to first bake it in the oven.

There are many thickening agents sold by grocers, but few of them are to be trusted; it is better to compound one's own, although it may take more time to do it.

Bread is an ingredient very largely used both in France and Switzerland in soup making; either put in the pot with the vegetables, and allowed to dissolve, or cut into dice and delicately browned in butter, then put in the tureen for the soup to be poured upon it, it forms a substantial addition to, and greatly increases the nourishing properties of the " potage."

Now we come to consider the purées—true vegetable soups.

The first desideratum in the making of a successful purée is patience on the part of the cook, for upon the patient rubbing of all the ingredients through the sieve will hang all the quality of the soup. It is by no means labour spent in vain.

The most common vegetable soup is the kind known as " Soupe à la Bataille," as all the vegetables are supposed to be fighting with each other.

With many people this is a foundation soup, and is varied by adding a larger quantity of the particular vegetable which is to give it its name for the day—more peas, if it is called pea soup, etc.

In the south of France a vegetable purée will have nothing but a little onion and a few savoury herbs added to its main ingredient.

Lentils, peas, haricots, beans, and potatoes are the most frequently used for purées. They are all rendered much richer and smoother to the taste if one or two beaten yolks of eggs are added the last thing before bringing to the table.

When a white soup is desired, milk or cream is added, and the latter should be made hot in a saucepan before putting into the tureen.

Turnips, chestnuts, potatoes, Jerusalem artichokes, vegetable marrows, and white haricot beans, all make most delicious white soup.

The vegetables are indeed few in number which are not pressed into the service of the soup pot in one form or another.

In green soups, where it is desirable to keep the colour nice, it is well to put the green vegetables in boiling water with a little salt added, and a grain of carbonate of soda, and let the cover of the pot be tilted to allow the steam to escape.

A delicate potage, and one which is considered a specific for indigestion by the good people of the south, is made as follows:—A good slice of white bread is cut into dice, and put in the tureen, four eggs, yolks and whites beaten separately; with the yolks four spoonfuls of olive oil are mixed, and this is poured over the bread.

A quart of water is boiled with a few shallots, a clove and a peppercorn or two, into this the beaten whites are stirred, and a few spoonsful of cold milk ; the whole is then poured into the tureen, and quickly mixed together.

This is called an " eau bouillie."

As there are but few things, whether of fish, flesh, fowl, or vegetables which will not lend themselves to soup making, given a fair intelligence with patience, industry, and cleanliness on the part of the cook, the variety is almost inexhaustible to the student of this branch of the profession.

Potato Soup.

For a quart of soup, boil three or four medium-sized potatoes, then mash them quite smooth, and put them into the stewpan with nearly the quantity of boiling water. Remove the outer skin from a large white onion, melt a small lump of butter, then slice the onion into it and let it stew until perfectly tender, but not brown. When done, dredge a little baked flour over, to absorb the butter, then stir this gradually into the boiling liquor; add salt and pepper to season it well, and let it boil gently until required. Just before pouring into the tureen stir in two tablespoonfuls of hot cream, and a teaspoonful of dried and sifted parsley.

To improve the appearance of the soup, a whole carrot may be boiled at the same time as the potatoes, then cut into fancy shapes and rounds and added to the whole. The beaten yolk of an egg, and a little more butter, will make the soup very much richer.

Brown Onion Soup.

A little clear stock is required for this.

Skin two or three large onions, slice them as thinly as possible, and fry them until thoroughly tender and well browned in a little beef dripping. Drain them. Make the stock almost boiling hot in your stewpan. Mix a little baked flour with the dripping in the frying pan, stir it over the fire to brown it. Add this gradually to the stock, see that it is perfectly smooth. Add the onions next, and leave it to simmer for half an hour. Remove all fat from the surface, add salt, pepper, a spoonful of sharp sauce, same of mushroom ketchup, and a drop of caramel if it be not brown enough already. Serve over fried croutons.

Tomato Soup.

Use either fresh or tinned tomatoes.

Melt two ounces of fresh butter, and frizzle first a few chopped shallots, or one white onion.

Next skin half a dozen fine tomatoes, and slice them into the butter, and stew them thus until quite dissolved. Have a quart of water, or the same quantity of clear broth, ready in the stewpan. When it boils throw in the white part of a slice of bread cut into dice. Add the contents of the smaller stewpan to this, let all simmer together for awhile, then pour through a strainer, rubbing the ingredients well that nothing good may be left behind.

Return to the stewpan, season it well, stir in the yolk of an egg beaten up in a cup of milk, let it nearly boil again, then serve.

Watercress Soup.

Boil half a pint of white haricots until thoroughly tender, rub them through a fine strainer, and add a quart of boiling water to the purée thus obtained.

Chop up quite finely a large bunch of washed and picked watercress,—and also a handful of green chives, a bunch of spring onions, some chervil, parsley, sorrel,—in fact anything green which you may be able to obtain.

Melt two ounces of fresh butter, frizzle the chopped green stuffs in this until they show signs of turning colour, then stir them briskly into the liquor in the stewpan. Season well.

The soup ought to be sufficiently thickened by the haricots, but if not, wet a teaspoonful of potato flour and stir that in, letting the liquor boil up once afterwards.

Vermicelli Soup.

Clear stock from mutton, beef or veal; pour boiling water over a small quantity of thin vermicelli; then drain it, and cut into short lengths with a sharp knife, and throw into the stock. Cut quite small one carrot, half a head of celery, and half a dozen fine leeks. Let these all boil until tender in a separate vessel; then add them to the stock, and season it well.

If macaroni be added instead of vermicelli, let it boil separately in a saucepan for twenty minutes; then drain and add to the stock.

Should it be preferred that the soup be thickened, use a spoonful of brown *roux* for the purpose; and cook the vegetables in a little clarified fat instead of water. Add the macaroni or vermicelli the last of all.

White Stock Soup.

A quart or more of stock made from knuckle of veal, chicken or ham bones. Boil an onion and a turnip in a small quantity of this stock; when tender, chop them up finely, and add them to the remainder of the clear liquor. Boil half a pint of fresh milk, and thicken it with a tablespoonful of potato flour previously wetted; stir it into the stock, season with salt, pepper, and a grate of nutmeg, and just before serving, stir in half an ounce of fresh butter.

Purée of Haricot Beans.

Let the beans soak over night; set them on with sufficient water to cover them, and boil them for three or four hours. Rub them through a sieve, leaving nothing but skins behind; to every pint of the purée thus obtained add a pint of boiling milk. Season liberally; chop a few shallots very finely, and cook them in a little butter; dredge a little flour over them to absorb the butter, then stir into the purée. Add a tablespoonful of cream before bringing to table.

When fresh "button" mushrooms are obtainable, a score of them may be skinned; then gently boiled for a minute or two, drained, and added to the soup.

Purée of Peas or Lentils.

Soak these also for a couple of hours. Boil them in the right quantity of water required for the soup. When beginning to dissolve, strain through a sieve as before, and return to the stewpan. Crumble a little stale roll into this liquor, and season with pepper and salt.

Chop finely half a dozen fresh spring onions or leeks, a bunch of fresh sweet herbs, and a few leaves of spinach. Cook these in a little butter, then stir into the purée.

Purée of Turnips and Parsnips.

Pare half a dozen sound white turnips, and half as many parsnips; add to them half a head of celery, a bunch of sweet herbs, half a dozen leeks, and an onion.

Boil all together in a quart of water for three hours. Strain and rub all well through a colander. Return to the pan; add enough boiling milk to make up the required quantity, season well, and stir in a tablespoonful of chopped parsley.

Jerusalem Artichoke Soup

is made very similarly to the above, substituting the artichokes for the turnips.

Purée of Carrots.

Use clear stock made from bones or shin of beef.

Grate a large carrot; chop finely a red onion, and skin two or three tomatoes. Let all these stew together in a covered vessel with a little clear beef dripping, until thoroughly cooked. Then stir them into the heated stock; skim off superfluous fat, season well, and crumble a French roll into the liquor. Let all come to boiling-point; then pour over a few fried croutons in the tureen.

Gamekeeper's Potage.

From the remains of game and poultry the following savoury soup may be made. Cut off any nice firm parts of meat, and reserve them for frying.

Make a stock from bones and trimmings, adding carrots, turnips, onions, herbs, and whole peppercorns to the pot; let this cook many hours. Strain the stock and remove all fat. Cut the meat into small neat pieces; roll in reasoned flour, and brown them well in a frying-pan.

Place the meat in the stock, and let that merely simmer. Frizzle a minced onion in the same fat until brown, then dredge a little baked flour over, sprinkle with salt, add a pinch of dried sage, and a drop of caramel; stir these into the stock, then let all simmer for half an hour, and serve at once.

It should be of the consistency of cream, highly seasoned, and of a light brown colour.

A spoonful of vinegar is a great improvement to thickened and much seasoned soups.

All soups should be seasoned sufficiently before taking them to table; it is most objectionable to find them requiring salt before they can be eaten at all.

CHAPTER III.

Vegetables and Vegetable Dishes.

VEGETABLES, as a rule, are not sufficiently appreciated amongst English people, neither are they cultivated in the quantity
and variety, nor exposed for sale with the
cleanliness and care which make this part of
a continental market so attractive to visit.

A well prepared dish of vegetables tempt-
ingly arranged, with an eye to contrast of
colour, may often be served in place of a dish
of meat; particularly in large families would it
be found most economical, sparing the joint,
and frequently obviating the necessity for a
second dish of meat; or if served cold, as a
salad, will prove a most acceptable accompaniment where cold meat is a dreaded dish.

The medicinal virtues of fresh, well-dressed
vegetables are great; they are blood purifiers,

as well as being easy of digestion, and most nutritious.

If freshly gathered out of the garden, they should be washed as they are wanted, and not allowed to remain in water; but when bought in town, it is often needful not only to wash, but to soak them in water for some time, to regain something of their original freshness.

If not the happy possessor of a bit of garden ground (and it is wonderful, with careful management, how much may be got out of ever so small a piece), it is a wise plan to treat with a farmer or cottage gardener for a regular supply.

To buy in shops or of costermongers is not cheap, besides the certainty that your purchase has suffered considerable handling before it reached you.

If laid on the floor of a cool cellar, taking care they do not touch each other, and are not wet at the time, vegetables may be kept quite good for a week in summer time; but in the autumn, when the crops are gathered in, a frugal housewife will lay in her store: carrots, turnips, parsnips, beetroot, potatoes, and such-like are best kept in dry sand.

Celery and leeks keep quite fresh if put in a

box of earth; onions should be strung together, and hung up.

In nearly all dishes and soups made of vegetables, herbs play an active part, particularly sorrel and parsley.

During spring and summer they are easily obtained fresh, but for winter use the parsley should be dried in bunches, as likewise a supply of mint, thyme, marjoram, sage, and, in fact, any herb you can procure.

The secret of keeping dried herbs a good colour is to dry them very quickly and thoroughly, hang them as near the kitchen stove as possible; when dry, rub them through a tamis, and bottle for use.

Sorrel is gathered in large quantities, and boiled like spinach, with coarse salt, then kept in a deep stone jar.

In cooking vegetables, it is most important to keep them a good colour, particularly in cooking "greens."

To do this, it is needful always to place them in boiling salt and water, and leave the lid of the saucepan slightly tilted, to let the steam escape.

For white vegetables, such as turnips, cauliflowers, salsifies, etc., the same precautions should be observed, and a little vinegar be added to the water.

A French cook will frequently take these out of the water when only partly cooked, and let them finish by simmering them in white sauce; this keeps them a very good colour indeed.

Any vegetables if cooked *more* than the proper time will soon become soddened; they should be lifted out of the water the moment they are done.

And now we come to consider vegetable dishes proper.

Here there is scope for much of taste and judgment, and the artistic eye of the *lady* cook as well as the skilled hand of the professional, for upon the arrangement of colour depends much of the success of the dish.

Take, for instance, a "plat de carrottes," with its pretty contrast of white and red and green, or the creamy whiteness of "choufleurs à la crême," and the very pretty dish of spinach with the white and yellow eggs reposing on their dark green bed, and say if it is not so.

The "garniture" of these dishes will call for as much taste as the arrangement of a bouquet.

Finely chopped parsley is the cook's grand resource in nearly all these compounds, and truffles, capsicums, eggs, even flowers, all are pressed into the service of ornamentation.

As it is the custom in France to serve most vegetables as a separate course, quite as much care is given to their preparation as to a course of meat, and various are the forms they are made to make; the sauces which accompany or disguise them, and the dressings which, if served cold, transform them into delicious salads.

A green vegetable, or "dish of greens," served as an English cook sends them to table, would in a French cuisine be considered quite an anomaly; there they would, after being well drained, be tossed up in butter, seasoned, some fragrant herbs added, and, generally, fried bread would be sent up with them.

Peas, haricots, broad beans, cabbages, and cauliflowers are certainly improved by this treatment, so are potatoes; and white sauce, either with or without parsley, is a frequent accompaniment to these and many other kinds of vegetables. Some, again, after being partially boiled, are fried in batter, as salsify and parsnips; these make an excellent luncheon or supper dish.

When onions are used, they should be first

lightly and quickly browned in fat, then drawn away from the fire, and allowed to cook slowly under cover; this draws the juices out, and makes them very much more easy of digestion.

Vegetables, if added to " ragouts " of meat, make them very much more savoury, and greatly economise the amount of meat. Carrots accord best with beef, turnips and parsnips best with mutton and veal, while tomatoes suit all meats.

Remnants of cold meat, which are often a source of perplexity to the economical housekeeper, may, with a judicious use of very simple means, be turned into many a delicious dish.

Green artichokes and asparagus are delicious, and do not come within the reach of the poor man, except he have a garden; but Jerusalem artichokes are both cheap and delicate, also very nourishing. Mushrooms, either stewed or broiled, are the delight of all classes, and well replace a dish of meat.

The forms which potatoes may be made to assume are almost legion; while a good potato may be spoiled by bad cooking, an inferior one may, with proper management, be rendered comparatively good.

P.C.   D

Large quantities of this most useful vegetable are constantly wasted in many families, owing to the way in which they are dressed.

How is it that the stalls of the " marchand de pommes-de-terre frites " are never seen in England, while they are so common in France, where they do a thriving trade ?

Vegetables are not usually associated with " sweet dishes "; but the cook who has once succeeded in making a vegetable plum-pudding, will find it a formidable rival to her very best and most time-honoured recipe.

It is an open secret that turnips and vegetable marrows are in great request in the large jam and marmalade factories ; and it is really surprising how readily these two vegetables adapt themselves to this sort of use, having the faculty of absorbing whatever flavour is added to them.

Many of the following recipes are distinctively French, and only those vegetables which have not been treated of elsewhere will be found here mentioned.

Sea Kale in Cream.

Boil sea kale in salted water until it is just tender, then drain it and lay in a dish, and cover with white sauce; or, better still, let the kale only be par-boiled, and finish cooking it in the sauce, stirring a cupful of cream into the latter at the last.

Before sea kale is in the market, a very similar dish to the above may be made by boiling a head of celery, and dressing it the same way. Use only the whitest parts.

Green Artichokes, "à la Barigoule."

For large-sized artichokes :—

Cut off the stalks and remove the tips from the leaves. Boil them in salted water until tender, then drain them, and press between a cloth to exclude all water.

Mix together a tablespoonful of sausage meat with as much butter, a few bread-crumbs, a spoonful of flour, the same of minced herbs, and a little seasoning. Stir this mixture over the fire for about five minutes, then carefully fill in the spaces between each leaf of the artichokes with it, and place them side by side in a shallow stewpan; pour a little butter or clarified fat over them, and bake quickly for five minutes.

Lift them out on to a dish; mix a spoonful of sharp sauce with the butter, and pour over all.

Green artichokes, after boiling, are commonly served with dissolved butter; or if cold with a *"sauce poivrade"* (see Chapter V.). The following way is also excellent :—

Remove the stalks, split each one in two, and boil them for five minutes.

Make a rich brown sauce from a little clear stock and brown *roux*; add to it one onion, a bunch of herbs, and glassful of white wine; season well.

Put the artichokes into this; cover up, and stew for an hour. Strain the sauce, place the artichokes in the middle of the dish, and pour the sauce around them.

Jerusalem Artichokes, à la Maître-d'hotel.

Wash the artichokes, and put them to boil in salted water with the skins on. When tender enough for a skewer to penetrate them, drain away the water, peel them, and cut into short, thick pieces. Have ready two ounces of butter melted; put the artichokes into it, turn them about, and sprinkle them with pepper and chopped parsley. When slightly frizzled serve them up. A dash of vinegar is an improvement.

Jerusalem Artichokes in Sauce.

After washing and paring them, boil them in water containing vinegar and salt until tender, then serve in white or brown sauce, or *sauce poulette*, according to discretion.

Cauliflowers au Gratin.

Boil them as if for eating with white sauce; drain and crush them with a fork, add a few bread-crumbs or a little cooked macaroni, a nob of butter, a cupful of cream, and plenty of pepper and salt. Butter a shallow dish, pour the mixture into it, sprinkle the surface with bread-crumbs, and bake until slightly browned.

Cauliflower "au Fromage."

Boil a large white cauliflower; drain it, and break it carefully into two parts.

Make a small quantity of good white sauce, and stir into it a spoonful of grated Parmesan, and a pinch of cayenne pepper.

Butter a fancy dish which will stand firing; break up half the cauliflower into small bits, and put at the bottom of the dish, cover with a layer of the sauce.

Place the other half of the cauliflower on top

of this; well cover every part of it with the remainder of the sauce; sprinkle it with more cheese, pour a little melted butter the last thing over the whole, and place the dish in the oven to brown the surface.

Fried Salsify.

Scrape the salsify, and throw them into vinegar and water to preserve the colour; boil them until just tender in strong salt and water.

Drain them, flour each one, then dip them into a batter, and drop them into boiling fat. Fry until brown; lift them carefully out and serve very hot, garnished with parsley.

Salsifies, when boiled, may be served in white or brown sauce, or cut small and added to stews of meat.

Asparagus tops à la Crème.

This is for very thin, green asparagus; the finer kinds with thick fleshy stalks are invariably served with the accompaniment of pure melted butter or white sauce; or, if cold, the cruet containing salt, pepper, vinegar, and oil is passed round to each individual partaking of them.

Cut the asparagus into inch lengths; leave

out all the white part, throw the pieces into boiling water for about two minutes, then drain, place them in a stewpan with butter, a lump of sugar, some pepper, and a teacupful of water; cover up and let them stew for at least an hour. Remove the onion, and thicken the sauce with the yolk of an egg and a little cream. Serve hot over a thin slice of fried bread.

Petits Pois.

Throw the shelled peas into boiling salted water for one or two minutes, not more; then drain them.

Dissolve a little butter at the bottom of a stewpan; put in the peas, two small onions, a sprig of mint and parsley, sprinkle with pepper; add a lump of sugar, and finally cover the top with a cabbage lettuce cut in half, and pour in half a teacupful of water. Put on the lid, and simmer the whole for nearly an hour. Remove the lettuce, herbs, and onions, and serve the peas with the sauce as it is, or thicken the latter by the addition of a yolk of egg and cream.

The above is for peas when served alone; when intended for accompanying meat, use a little of the fat from the joint, and omit the thickening agents.

Stuffed Cucumbers.

Prepare a mince from the remains of cold meat, poultry, or fish; season it highly, and make it moist with gravy. If a purely vegetarian stuffing be desired, make it of breadcrumbs, parsley and chives, butter and seasoning, and moisten with a beaten egg.

Pare a short thick cucumber, and with a corer remove all the seedy interior; press the stuffing into it until it be quite full. Melt a good-sized lump of butter in a stewpan, place the cucumber in it (if it will not go in without, cut it in two), put in an onion and a bunch of herbs, also a cup of water; cover up and stew gently for an hour or so. Remove to a dish, take out the onion and herbs, thicken the butter with a little potato flour, season it, add a spoonful of chopped parsley and a few drops of vinegar; let it boil, then pour over the cucumbers.

Aubergines Farcies.

Though but rarely seen, this vegetable is a most delicious one.

Pare each one, and split them down lengthwise; remove the soft interior part.

Melt a little butter, and place the half aubergines to simmer in this. When slightly browned, remove them to a fireproof dish, and stir into the butter a teaspoonful of flour and a few spoonfuls of gravy. Chop up the portions which were removed from the insides; add a good spoonful of fresh herbs minced and salt and pepper to them, then mix in with the sauce. Let this cook awhile, then fill up the cavities of the aubergines, sprinkle the surface with breadcrumbs, place a few bits of butter in the dish, and bake quickly for ten minutes.

Serve in the same dish.

Grilled Aubergines.

Split them lengthwise, and steep them in salad oil for ten minutes, then drain them, and sprinkle with salt and pepper, and broil them over the fire, turning on both sides.

Aubergines may also be split and fried; also baked simply with butter.

Fried Parsley

is not as frequently used as it should be; for garnishing hot pastry or fried dishes it should always be used in preference to fresh. Place the picked sprigs in a frying-basket, and plunge that for exactly one minute into boiling fat.

Curried Vegetables.

The following vegetables all make excellent curries, and this form of serving vegetables makes a pleasant variation, besides being a very savoury one. The addition of a little dessicated cocoanut (purchasable from any grocer in tins) gives a delicacy to the flavour.

Potatoes, celery, onions, turnips, parsnips, artichokes, haricots, broad beans, vegetable marrows, and cucumbers.

For a *brown* curry proceed as follows :—

Have ready some hot fat, enough to fry the vegetables with ease.

Have the latter cut in slices or small even-sized pieces; fry them until brown and tender through; sprinkle them all over with a little curry powder, and add sufficient salt. If you have no brown thickening ready made, dredge the vegetables with a little baked flour before they leave the frying-pan; then pour in a good cupful of clear stock, a spoonful of "Nabob" or other sharp sauce and ketchup, a pinch of cocoanut, and half the juice of a lemon.

Let all simmer together for several minutes, then serve in the same way as a meat curry.

For a *white* curry, cook the vegetables in water previous to cutting them up. Make a small quantity of rich white sauce.

Dissolve a little butter in a stewpan; put the vegetables in to become well heated through, but not to brown; pepper them with curry powder; stir in the sauce, then just before serving add a little cream.

Vegetable Pies.

As in curries, a combination of different vegetables produces a better result than any one kind used singly; also the seasoning must not be given too sparingly.

Most vegetables for pies should be at least partly cooked beforehand, and onions are more rich in flavour if previously *fried*. A sprinkling of tapioca, sago, etc., gives smoothness and " body " to the pie.

Seasonings should consist of pepper, salt, fine herbs (dried or fresh), cayenne, mace, allspice, and sometimes grated cheese.

As a rule the vegetables should be placed in separate layers, the seasoning between, and the dish filled up with water, stock, or milk, according to discretion; then simmered a little while

before putting on the crust. Make and ornament the crust as if for a meat pie.

The following combinations go excellently
well together.

Alternate layers of cooked macaroni, frizzled
onions, green peas, and tomatoes (the latter
uncooked); season with pepper, salt, mint and
lemon juice.

Alternate layers of cooked haricot beans and
mushrooms, with a few bits of butter and some
chopped parsley; pepper and salt for seasoning.

Alternate layers of potatoes, onions, and
apples (all uncooked); season with pepper, salt,
and mace.

Tomatoes, cooked macaroni, onions, apples,
and grated cheese.

Potatoes, hard-boiled eggs, fresh herbs, spring
onions, and parsley.

Cooked broad beans, frizzled onion, parsley,
seasoning, and tapioca, filled up with milk.

Cooked celery, turnips, and boiled rice. The
water in which the celery was cooked is thickened, and a little cream added to it, plenty of
pepper and salt, a little grated cheese, if liked,
and the dish filled up with this.

CHAPTER IV.

Salads.

THE subject of salads reminds one of Sydney Smith's truly Epicurean recipe for a salad dressing, which he concludes by saying—

> " 'Twould tempt the dying anchorite to eat.
> Back to the world he'd turn his weary soul,
> And plunge his fingers in the salad bowl."

This well-known recipe of his is, however, quite beyond the reach of an ordinary family salad maker, though well deserving of attention when a festival calls for extra care in regard to this portion of the repast.

There are but few days in the year when the salad bowl is absent from the table of the *bon bourgeois*. He follows the order which kindly nature has provided for him with faithfulness through the succeeding seasons.

Spring and summer bring the true "salad days" of his existence, wherein he may revel in

the variety open to his choice, and unless the
frost be too unkind, he will manage to preserve
his curly endives till the dainty *coquille*
has appeared above ground; then watercress
speedily comes to ring the changes with dande-
lion and chicory.

Indeed, there are few things in the vegetable
kingdom which do not lend themselves to his
skilful dressing; even cold meat, fish and game
he will treat in this manner with much effect.

In warm weather, cold meat sent to table in
this way, or served with the salad as an accompaniment, is often far more acceptable than a
hot joint.

An old Spanish proverb says it takes four
persons to make a successful salad : a spend-
thrift to throw in the oil, a miser to drop in the
vinegar, a lawyer to administer the seasoning,
and a madman to stir the whole together.

Though comparatively a simple thing to prepare, it is very easily spoiled if regard be not
paid to one or two golden rules. The main
thing to observe in lettuce and vegetable salads
is that they should be as dry as possible, and
the dressing be added at the last moment only.

It is better not to wash lettuces, but to wipe
them with a clean towel, then shred them into

the bowl. If muddy or gritty, or a trifle stale, let them lie in cold water awhile, then shake vigorously in one of the open wire baskets sold for the purpose.

Vegetables, such as beans, haricots, peas, etc., and kidney beans, should, after boiling, be quite cold and thoroughly well drained before using; plenty of chopped parsley, and a suspicion of onion added to them when placed in the bowl.

Amongst the vegetables appropriate for salads in addition to the first-mentioned, are asparagus, artichokes, boiled beetroot, celery, cucumber, tomatoes, cauliflowers, dandelions, French beans, lentils, broad beans, radishes, salsifies, chicory, and watercress, mustard and cress, chives, and a variety of herbs, which, served with the others, give piquancy to the flavour, and aid digestion.

A few shreds of onion should never be forgotten, though French people prefer to use a clove of garlic, and rub the inside of the bowl with it.

A salad well prepared and *garnished* is a most charming compound. For the garnishing, only such things as can be eaten with the mixture should be used, such as bright radishes, sliced beetroot and cucumber, hard-boiled eggs; nasturtium leaves and flowers and marigolds may also be used. Both the latter flowers are edible, and have a pleasant flavour.

Of meat salads, chicken salad, or mayonnaise, is the most commonly known, but most poultry and game may be treated in this way.

A very appetising way of treating the remains of cold beef is to cut it into dice, excluding all fat and gristle (a very small piece of meat is needed), then to add a good tablespoonful of chopped parsley and chives, and dress as a salad with mustard and oil and vinegar; this goes by the name of a " persillade."

Fish, too, such as cold salmon or turbot, halibut and cod, with lobster, either by itself or as a garniture to the first-named, all four being treated in this manner; eggs should always be included in the dressing. The coral of a lobster is most valuable as a decoration.

Lettuce and watercress salads are invariably served with omelettes and most other dishes made with eggs; and with hot meat and gravy they are a delicious accompaniment, many people, particularly gentlemen, preferring them thus instead of to cold meat.

Joan Cromwell's grand salad was composed of equal parts of almonds, raisins, capers,

pickled cucumbers, shrimps, and boiled turnips !

Although a salad should not be dressed until
the moment it is required to be eaten, the dressing may be prepared some hours before it is
needed for use, and, where time is precious, and
salads are frequently required, sufficient for two
or three days' supply may be prepared at once,
and bottled up ready for use.

If you would succeed and have a truly delicious salad, *make your own dressing*; let no
hands but your own have anything to do with
compounding it. Above all, eschew the compounds sold at the grocers under the name of
" creams " or " salad dressing."

A foolish prejudice exists among many people
against salad oil, but when once they have over-
come the dislike, they generally end by becoming very partial to it ; its judicious use is of
great benefit, as it tends to prevent the fermen·
tation caused in the stomach by the presence of
a raw vegetable, and is a corrective to flatu-
lence.

It can often be taken in salads by invalids for
whom cod-liver oil has been prescribed, which
is so disagreeable and difficult to take, and is
found to be very nearly as nourishing.

P.C.   E

There are different oils procurable to suit all
tastes, but the purest olive oil is always preferred by both French and Swiss people, and is
bought by them in large flagons, straight from
the growers.

The *principles* of salad-making having been
broadly given in the foregoing remarks, recipes
for a few choice salads are here appended.

Capsicum Salad.

An excellent digestive.

The capsicums should be rather unripe,
although for appearance sake they should be
red in colour.

Split them, remove the seeds, let them lie in
cold water for some hours, to reduce their
pungency.

With the fingers pull them to small pieces,
and shred some crisp lettuce also. Chop a
small onion finely, and slice up two or three
tomatoes.

Mix all together in the salad bowl; sprinkle
with salt, then pour several spoonfuls of oil and
one of vinegar over all, and mix the whole very
thoroughly together.

Cucumber Salad.

There will be none of the usual grumbling as to the indigestibility of cucumbers if the following directions are minutely followed :—

Firstly, slice the cucumbers as thinly as a sheet of notepaper, leaving the rind on if the taste of it be not disliked ; place the slices on a plate, also some finely shred onions, half as many as the cucumber ; cover with a sprinkling of salt, then with another plate, and let these stand for half an hour to " cry." Then drain the " tears " away, and put cucumbers and onions into the salad bowl. Dredge with pepper and a little castor sugar, then pour over the usual proportion of oil and vinegar, and *serve at once.*

When this salad is to accompany fish, leave out the onion, and substitute a few sprigs of watercress.

Carrot Salad.

An accompaniment to cold salt beef.

Slice thinly some carrots which have been boiled whole and allowed to become cold. Lay the slices separately on a flat dish and season them with pepper, salt, and a drop of oil on each ; squeeze some lemon juice over them.

Shred finely some lettuce, and mix some

chopped chives or shallots with it, and nearly fill the bowl with this. Dredge with the usual dressing, and mix lightly. Carefully lift the slices of carrot and lay them over the green; decorate with tufts of scraped horse-radish and sprigs of watercress.

Celery Salad.

The white stalks of celery should be shred downwards, then cut into inch lengths, and piled in the centre of a shallow glass dish.

Pour over these a *cream* salad dressing, and place a tuft of the green leaves on the top. Make a border round the base of pickled red cabbage, a few strips of hard-boiled egg, and an outer edge of celery leaves.

Apple Salad.

A tasty accompaniment to cold roast pork, goose or raised pie.

Keswicks are the best for this purpose, on account of their sharp juiciness and fine green skins. Core the apples, but leave the skins on. Slice them on to a shallow dish, dust them with cayenne pepper, and sprinkle among them a few finely minced shallots. Place a few split capsicums and tiny pickled gherkins about the edge, strain a little lemon juice, and mix it with an equal quantity of salad oil, and a pinch each of salt and powdered sugar. Pour over the apples, and serve before they have time to change colour.

Bean Salad. *(Salade de Haricots Verts.)*

French beans are by far the best for making this, although kidney beans are not at all bad if treated in the same way.

When the former are used, strip the strings off and simply break the beans in inch lengths ; do not cut them. Boil them until tender ; drain thoroughly, and leave until quite cold. Put them in a bowl, sprinkle with about two table-spoonfuls of finely chopped parsley and any fresh herbs obtainable, then with salt and pepper, and dress with vinegar and oil. Serve immediately.

Fennel Salad.

For accompanying white fish, turbot, cod, halibut or hake.

Use only the tender sprouts of the fennel, and shred them finely ; intersperse these with shred leaves of tender cabbage lettuce.

Pile up in the bowl, and garnish with chopped

hard-boiled egg, shreds of fresh lemon, and chopped pickled walnut. Dress as preferred.

Haricot Bean Mayonnaise.

The white haricot beans should have been soaked previous to cooking them, to ensure their being thoroughly mealy afterwards.

When well drained, mix with them a little mustard and cress, and the faintest suspicion of raw onion.

Pour over all a good mayonnaise or cream dressing.

Very nice for luncheon with brown bread and butter.

Mushroom Salad.

Small or "button" mushrooms should be used for this.

Remove the outer skins and most of the stalk, drop them into boiling salted water, and boil gently for two or three minutes. Remove them on to a cloth. When quite cold, sprinkle them with mixed pepper and salt, and chopped parsley. Pile in the salad bowl, and dredge liberally with oil and spiced vinegar.

Potato Salad.

Slice some cold boiled potatoes very evenly, sprinkle them all over with finely minced parsley and shallots, and strew a little thinly sliced lemon amongst them. Mix a teaspoonful of grated horse-radish with an egg salad dressing, and pour it over. Decorate with sliced beet-root, pickled walnuts, and sprigs of watercress.

Sardine Salad.

Shred finely some crisp curly endive, dredge it with pepper and salt, some lemon juice, and the oil of the sardines. Mix very thoroughly, then pile in the centre of a round glass dish. Border with thin circles of hard-boiled eggs. Take several unbroken sardines; split them open to remove the bone, and sprinkle them with fresh lemon peel and cayenne pepper; close them up, then sharply cut each sardine into three pieces. Lay these fillets over the top of the prepared endive, and serve.

A sausage salad might be made in similar fashion, using slices of Lyons or Bologna sausage cut in fancy shapes. The dressing should have mustard and the yolk of egg added to the other ingredients.

Game Salads.

Almost any kind of cold game may be dressed as a salad, and the following general directions will do for all :—

The meat must be very thinly sliced—shaved, in fact—in neat pieces. Lettuces, mustard and cress, and any salad herbs obtainable should be arranged in the bowl in alternate layers with the game. Dress with a mixture of chutney and oil, with a little spiced vinegar, and decorate the surface with chopped jelly.

Ham Salad.

Cold boiled or baked *smoked* ham is the best, although unsmoked may be used.

Mix together and put into a fine dredger a small quantity each of celery salt, cayenne and black pepper, white sugar and allspice.

Shave the lean of the ham, and squeeze lemon juice over the pieces, then lightly dredge them with the above mixture.

Shave up some white onions and celery, and put them in the salad bowl with a few white lettuce hearts. Add the ham next, then pour several spoonfuls of oil over all and a dash of vinegar. Serve quickly.

Lobster Salad.

Mix a well varied green salad, and add the flakes taken from the larger part of the lobster; make a pyramid of this.

Dress with a rich cream dressing, containing a spoonful of anchovy sauce; then decorate in the following order, commencing from the base : beetroot, sliced cucumber, eggs sliced, prawns, eggs, and lobster coral at the top.

As before advised, make your own "salad dressing," whether it be simple or compound.

The many mixtures which come under this heading are after all compounded of a few things, a greater or smaller proportion of each being employed, according as fancy or fashion dictates.

The following are the components of all salad dressings,—the first five being the most commonly used :—

Ground pepper, black or white.

Salt and celery salt.

Mustard.

Salad or olive oil.

Vinegar, plain, spiced, or flavoured.

Yolk of egg, raw or pounded.

Mashed potato.

Lemon juice.
Sauces : tomato, anchovy, Worcester, etc.
Curry powder.
Powdered sugar.
Horse-radish.
Cream and milk.

Rules for Mixing the Dressings.

Add all liquids slowly.

Put in the vinegar at the last.

Mix very thoroughly, and if intended for future use, keep in air-tight bottles, in a cool dark place.

Shake well before using.

CHAPTER V.

Sauces.

A GENERAL knowledge of sauces is a part of every intelligent housekeeper's culinary education. They are no longer the appendages of the rich man's table only, for by their aid the homeliest dish may become "fit to set before a king," although the actual cost is within the compass of the peasant's purse.

The great *chef* Soyer used to say that sauces are to cookery what grammar is to language, or the gamut is to music. However this may be, the skill of a cook is shown in nothing more assuredly than in the way she manufactures a sauce.

Sauce certainly ought to serve either as a relish or a finish to the dish it accompanies. The most homely fare may be made relishing, as the most excellent may be improved, by a well-made sauce, just as the most perfect oil-painting is improved by varnishing.

Sauces should display a decided character. Many cooks make a grand mistake on this point; they think they cannot make a sauce sufficiently savoury without putting into it everything that happens to be available, supposing every addition must be an improvement.

Spices, herbs, etc., are often absurdly jumbled together. Why have cloves and allspice, mace, and nutmeg in the same sauce, or onions, garlic, and shallots all together? Any one of these is sufficient by itself.

You might as well, to make soup, order one quart of water from the New River, one from the Thames, a third from Hampstead, and a fourth from Chelsea.

An ingenious cook will form as endless a variety of compositions as a musician with his seven notes, or a painter with his pigments; no part of her business offers a more frequent opportunity for the display of her imagination; but to become a perfect mistress in the art of cleverly extracting flavours, besides the gift of good taste, requires all the experience and skill of the accomplished professor.

Hot sauces should be sent to table as hot as

possible; and when wine or thickening has been added, they should be allowed to boil up again, so that the flavours may be well blended.

In compound sauces the flavouring should be so nicely proportioned that no one should predominate over the other, but that the mixture give out a mellow flavour which cannot but be acceptable to the most critical gourmand.

Although classed among the elegancies of cookery, they are not necessarily extravagant, or they would never form so important a part of the *menu* of our *bonne bourgeoise*.

With her, even the juice that runs from the meat is "sauce," for it is seldom or never served on the meat dish, as it is in England. That she would consider wasteful, but carefully pouring off every drop, by a few skilful additions it is "lengthened," and then served in a *saucière*.

Stock forms the foundation of nearly all meat sauces, as it is easily adapted to whatever colour is desired.

If clear, bright sauce, which is also to be thick, is required, the stock should be thickened with potato flour, as that is transparent, and wine—either golden sherry or port—is usually added.

For a thick sauce not necessarily clear, there

are many ways of thickening; brown roux,
which a good cook will make for herself, and
keep by her, is most preferable.

Vegetable juice is the most wholesome colouring matter; spinach juice as a green when
available, or a good substitute is to be found in
crushed parsley.

A most delicious sauce is made from fresh
tomatoes, for serving hot with boiled beef or
veal; and when fresh ones are not to be had,
the tinned or preserved ones will do for the
purpose.

They should be frizzled in butter, seasoned,
then just covered with good bouillon, a few
tiny shallots and a little fragrant "bouquet"
added to them, and allowed to simmer for
an hour, after which it is passed through a
strainer.

Slices of cold beef or veal laid in this sauce,
and allowed to get thoroughly hot through,
with a few bits of lean ham or bacon, then
dished with finely chopped parsley sifted over
all, makes a very capital way of finishing up a
joint.

A thin clear "sauce piquante" is "sauce à la
Diable," into the composition of which enter
shallots and several herbs finely mixed, made

mustard, horse-radish grated, salt and pepper, vinegar and oil or butter, well stewed together, and a little stock, brown thickening and wine added.

In all brown sauces, the principal ingredients will be found to be, roughly stated, shallots, carrots, mushrooms, yolks of eggs, herbs, parsley, garlic, cloves, pepper, mustard, vinegar and oil; sometimes white or red wine, with thickening material as required.

When making sauces for game and poultry, the goodness should be thoroughly extracted from the giblets and all available bones, by crushing and thoroughly stewing. The pinch of salt must not be omitted in any sauce.

White sauces form quite a catalogue by themselves, from the simple white sauce made from thickened milk to the somewhat elaborate " béchamel sauce."

For a good white sauce—which is also the foundation of the richer kinds of the same—use a tablespoonful of flour mixed with a little water, and an ounce of butter and milk or cream to the amount required. When this is boiled, it can receive whatever addition is to give it character to suit the dish it accompanies —capers, parsley, anchovies, oysters, shrimps, spices, lemons; in fact, it can be varied *ad libitum.*

Where many sauces are required, it is a great economy of time and material to have a supply of both brown and white *roux* at hand. Hastily made *roux* is impossible; and no mixture of flour and butter or other thickening agent can fill its place—certainly not in taste, and really not in appearance.

Equal quantities of pure butter and *baked* flour, stirred briskly and steadily over the fire for a longer or shorter time, is the one and only way of making *roux*; the difference in colour depends entirely on the time expended upon the task.

Sauce dite Beurre Noir.

Melt a fairly large lump of butter in a saucepan, and keep it briskly stirred while it changes colour; let it become quite brown, but not burnt. Throw in a handful of lightly chopped parsley, a pinch of pepper, and a spoonful of vinegar.

Black butter sauce is frequently served with fish.

Sauce Piquante.

Chop a shallot finely, and frizzle it in a little butter; add a tablespoonful of brown *roux*, a teaspoonful of made mustard, same of mixed salt and pepper, a tablespoonful of vinegar, and half a pint of warm water. Boil together, then strain through a sieve, and lastly throw in a tablespoonful of chopped gherkins.

Sauce Robert.

A spoonful of brown *roux*, half a pint of clear stock, plenty of seasoning, and a teaspoonful of mustard added last of all.

Frequently served with cutlets and steaks, notably with pork.

There are two distinct kinds of white sauce— viz., *Sauce blanche Parisienne* and *Sauce blanche Normande.*

Parisienne.

Dissolve in a saucepan a small lump of butter, and work into it as much baked flour or potato flour as it will absorb; when smooth, add a few spoonfuls of water to it. When this boils, add to it a fresh quantity of butter cut in small pieces—enough to make the required quantity of sauce. Stir steadily until all is completely

dissolved, but do not let it boil again. The
juice of half or a whole lemon is added at the
last.

Normande.

Moisten a spoonful of *fécule* or flour with sufficient water, add to it a small lump of butter,
and milk, to make the requisite quantity; stir
over the fire until it boils freely, then season and
add lemon juice.

White *roux*, to which is added milk, or milk
and water, makes this sauce to perfection.

A little thick cream added at the last greatly
improves white sauce.

Sauce Poulette.

Make a white sauce according to either of the
above; allow an onion and a few herbs to simmer
in it for a while, then strain, and stir in the
beaten yolk of an egg.

Sauce Soubése.

Chop up finely a dozen or more shallots,
frizzle them slowly in a little butter, dredge a
little flour over them, then stir in a tumblerful of
hot water; let simmer for a little time. The
sauce may then be strained, or not, as desired,

but it should receive the addition of salt, pepper,
and a spoonful or two of cream.

Served with mutton.

Sauce Ravigote.

Hot.—Put into a saucepan a teacupful of water
or clear stock, add to it a spoonful each of
minced chives, shallots, chervil, tarragon, mustard
and cress, pepper and salt, and one of vinegar.
Boil these together for five minutes, then stir in
a small lump of butter, and a teaspoonful of
potato flour wetted with water to thicken it.

Cold.—Take the same herbs, after mincing
them, and pound them in a mortar; add to them
the raw yolk of an egg. Mix well together,
and add, drop by drop, three spoonfuls of salad
oil. A spoonful of vinegar and one of made
mustard are stirred in last of all.

Sauce Tartare.

Mix together the yolks of three eggs, a spoonful of mustard and one of vinegar, then add
slowly three spoonfuls of salad oil. Stir carefully over the fire until thoroughly hot, but it
must not reach boiling-point. Or it may be used
cold.

Sauce Bordelaise.

Melt a small piece of butter, and frizzle in that two sliced shallots; when done, either stir in a tablespoonful of brown *roux* or sufficient potato flour to absorb the butter. Add a teacupful of clear stock, a wineglassful of claret, two tablespoonfuls of tomato sauce, a pinch of salt, same of pepper, and boil together; stir a pinch of mixed herbs in at the last. Much liked with beefsteaks and cutlets.

Béchamel Sauce.

Some clear but highly flavoured stock is required for the foundation of this. Simmer in this a small onion, a bunch of sweet herbs, a carrot cut in rounds, and a clove. When required for use, strain through a muslin, thicken with one or two spoonfuls of white *roux*, let it boil up once, season well, and stir in lastly three tablespoonfuls of hot cream.

Sauce au Jambon.

Chop finely a few ounces of lean ham; frizzle it in a stewpan with a bit of butter. When cooked, stir in a sufficiency of potato flour to absorb the butter, and clear stock or warm water to reduce it to the consistency of cream. Put in a small bunch of herbs, and some pepper. Let all simmer for upwards of an hour, then strain through a tamis.

Excellent for serving with poached eggs, cooked celery, salsifies, etc.

Sauce Financière.

Put in a saucepan half a pint of good clear stock, a few fowl or game giblets; cut small pieces of cooked liver and ham, a dozen small mushrooms, a dozen shallots, two or three olives, stoned and cut small (or tomatoes may be used instead), a glass of white wine, a spoonful of scraped horse-radish, pepper and salt. Let all these simmer together for a couple of hours, then thicken the sauce with brown " roux " or butter and flour rolled together, add any gravy available and a small spoonful of curry powder. Boil it once more and serve.

Salmis,

For the remains of poultry or game.

Dissolve a lump of butter the size of an egg, stir into it a large tablespoonful of " fécule " or potato flour, stir together until brown; add a cupful of stock and one of red wine, salt, pepper and spices. Mix together well, and when it has boiled a few minutes draw the sauce away from the fire, and put in the joints and pieces to be gently simmered therein.

A Richer Salmis.

Crush the bones, necks, giblets, etc., of the birds which you have been jointing; put all together into a stewpan with red wine and stock enough to cover them, two or three onions, a carrot, pepper, spice and cloves. Stew them together a long time, then strain through a hair sieve. Thicken this sauce until it becomes the consistency of cream, add salt, and taste if it be rightly seasoned. Warm up the jointed birds in the sauce, pour on to a dish, and garnish with potato rissoles or fried croutons. Serve very hot.

Mayonnaise Blanche.

The chief ingredient of this sauce is a small quantity of clear, savoury jelly. The jelly should be gradually melted by warmth, but must not become warm itself. When sufficiently dissolved to allow of its whisking easily, set the basin containing it on the ice if possible, if not, in a very cold place. Add an equal quantity of

good salad oil to it, a spoonful or two of good
flavoured vinegar, and a little salt and pepper
mixed ; then proceed to whisk the whole to a
white creamy froth. The oil and vinegar are
better if added by degrees. Keep the mayonnaise very cold.

Mayonnaise Sauce.

This sauce is a mixture of yolks of eggs, oil,
and vinegar or lemon-juice.

Care is required in the mixing thereof; the oil
should be added to the beaten eggs by drops,
and the acid put in in the same way the last of
all.

The proportion usually observed is that of a
tablespoonful of oil to every egg-yolk, and a
few drops of vinegar. If found too thick when
finished, use a little cold water to bring it to the
requisite consistency. Use a wooden or silver
spoon in mixing a mayonnaise.

Green Mayonnaise Sauce

is made by adding a small quantity of finely
minced herbs—chervil, cress, parsley, etc.—
to plain mayonnaise.

Horse-radish Sauce.

Pare off the outer skin, then scrape or grate an ounce of horse-radish; slightly thicken a cupful of cream or cream and milk, put the horse-radish into it with half a teaspoonful of salt and a lump of sugar; make the sauce very hot, and just before bringing to table stir in a spoonful of vinegar or lemon juice.

Horse-radish Sauce,

For cold meat.

Scrape the root very finely; to two table-spoonfuls of it add half a teaspoonful of salt and a whole one of made mustard. Stir these into a ready mixed yolk of egg and oil, and add lastly a spoonful of vinegar. Serve in a sauce boat. Cream may be substituted for the egg and oil if preferred.

Sauce Parisienne,

For sweet puddings.

Mix a wineglassful of rum or sweet wine with the beaten yolks of three eggs and a tablespoon-ful of sugar; stir over the fire until the mixture begins to thicken, draw it aside and add to it three tablespoonfuls of cream. Keep warm, but do not let it boil.

Sauce Napolitaine,

For Neapolitan and custard puddings.

Dissolve four ounces of currant jelly in a saucepan with four lumps of sugar, add to this a wineglassful of claret or port wine. Make hot, but do not let it boil.

Sauce aux Citrons.

Peel two lemons and squeeze the juice from them. Place the rind with half a pint of water and four ounces of lump sugar, to boil in a saucepan. When the goodness has been extracted, remove the rind, stir in a teaspoonful of corn flour previously wetted with cold water, the lemon juice, and an ounce of butter; boil up once and serve in a tureen.

Sauce au Confiture.

Mix smoothly together an ounce of dissolved butter and the same quantity of flour; stir in half a pint of warm water with a pinch of salt. Boil this sauce well, then add to it three or four spoonfuls of nice jam, free from stones.

Flavoured Vinegars.

One or two small bottlesful of vinegars of different flavours will be found most useful for sauces and gravies.

As a rule, steep the herbs or roots in plain vinegar for about a fortnight, then strain the latter, put it on in a pan to boil for a short space, and when cold bottle for use.

Horse-radish, celery, chili, garlic, mushroom, and walnut vinegars are made from roots; tarragon, mint, sage, nasturtium, basil, etc., from herbs.

Fruit vinegars for sweet sauces, such as raspberry, blackberry, plum, etc., are made by steeping the fruit in the vinegar until all the colour and flavour of it has been drawn out, then straining the vinegar into an enamelled pan and boiling it with half its proportion of sugar. Boil for ten minutes, and bottle up well.

A very small quantity of flavoured vinegar is sufficient; it must not be used as freely as plain vinegar.

CHAPTER VI.

The "Daubière" or "Braisière."

THERE is a kind of stew very popular in France which is known as a "daube." "Bœuf à la daube" is a favourite dish, but veal, mutton, and particularly poultry, all lend themselves admirably to being treated in this way.

One great advantage it has is that inferior cuts of meat, or elderly (consequently tough) denizens of the poultry yard, are quite as eligible for use in this way as the finest and most tender; if anything, they are, indeed, preferable, as they are found to contain more flavour if they can be made tender, and the object of this process is to make them tender, in spite of all resistance they may offer.

The daubière is a close-covered stewing-pot of glazed earthenware, with a deep rim round the top for holding charcoal. It is put either in a corner of the oven, or placed over the grating on the charcoal stove, with more hot coals round the brim. The latter way is the true method of braising.

For cooking a large piece of meat—a leg of mutton, for instance, which can be left until cold before it is cut—it is a mode of cooking truly beyond compare. Most people remember the old rhyme anent the turkey :—

"Turkey boiled is turkey spoiled,
Turkey roast is turkey lost;
But for turkey braised, the Lord be praised !"

Any one who has once tasted turkey done in this way will well understand how it is so much superior.

This mode of cooking has for its special object to cause as little evaporation as possible, and thus to retain all the natural juices and flavour of the meat. What is not left in the meat is fixed in the jelly produced by it.

Large pieces or joints of meat cooked in this way are equally good eaten either hot or cold ; but, as before stated, inferior portions of meat, if stewed in this vessel, may be rendered most excellent and nutritious.

Let us first take " Bœuf à la daube." The portion of beef used for this is a slice—say, an inch thick—from the shoulder of beef ; either above the blade or under it will do.

Remove all bone and skin; if you get a proper slice, there will be little of either. Take a small portion of beef kidney, a slice of fat bacon or salted pork, and a few large white onions; cut the meat into small squares, the bacon into strips, the kidney into small pieces, and slice the onion finely.

Then in your daubière arrange them in layers, dredging a little flour over each layer of meat, and taking care to have the fat bacon for the final layer. A few peppercorns should be disposed about, and a very little salt. Then, last of all, a glass of red wine should be poured over. Give it three or four hours to cook. It is most excellent.

Veal done in this same manner should be left whole, the kidney omitted; but the meat should be liberally larded through with fat bacon, more placed round it, a clove or two and peppercorns, but no onions. Sweet herbs are an improvement, and white wine instead of red.

Of course the wine may be omitted altogether where great economy is to be observed; the daube will be less rich, but none the less good without it.

Legs of mutton, shanks, thick portions of the

shoulder, etc., require no addition, save a few sweet herbs and a little fat to give moisture. The same parts of lamb may be cooked in this way also, and the meat will be found to waste less if so treated.

True "bœuf à la mode" is cooked in the daubière. When intended to be eaten hot, the vegetables are served with the meat; but not so intended, they should be lifted out, and the fat over the gravy removed as far as possible, leaving the meat in the vessel until quite cold.

It is sometimes well to place a weight over the meat before replacing the lid; it will slice more evenly if this precaution be observed.

A piece of the leg of beef or the "round" cooked in this manner, and left till cold, makes a capital luncheon dish; it will absorb the flavour of vegetables, bacon, fat, etc., quite readily.

For cooking turkeys, geese or poultry, "en daube," the same general directions will suffice.

Choose an old bird by preference; pluck and empty it, saving the heart, liver, and gizzard, also the neck; scald these well. Singe the bird, and scald the inside, then truss as if for roasting.

Place some fat bacon or salt pork at the bot-

tom of the daubière, your bird upon that, and
pack round it the giblets, a calf's foot split and
quartered, two or three carrots split and quartered, an onion, some bay-leaves, thyme, and
parsley. Add peppercorns and a little salt, a
cupful of good stock, and a glass of wine if
liked ; then cover up tightly, and cook gently
for five or six hours.

If intended to be eaten cold, the bird should
be lifted out, the liquor strained off into a
saucepan, and allowed to boil gently until reduced to one-third; then all fat must be removed, and a white of egg added to clarify it.

When nearly cold, the bird may be carefully
coated all over with this glaze. Garnished
with curled parsley, it is a handsome dish, and
no fear need be felt as to whether it will prove
tender or no.

The giblets and vegetables would be served
with the bird if eaten hot; in any case, they
make an appetising little dish by themselves
with a little of the gravy.

A ham may be successfully braised in this
vessel, and thus cooked it will be found to
retain far more flavour than if it were boiled.

It goes without saying that it requires
nothing with it save a little water. The juice

which runs from it, with the addition of a little gelatine and white of egg, will make the glaze for ornamenting it.

In the South it is customary, after the meat is cooked, to lift it out on to the dish, and then to put in whatever vegetables are intended to be eaten with it ; say, for example, a leg of mutton has been cooked in the daubière, and it is intended to have a dish of haricots or flageolets to accompany it; these last will have been boiled until tender, then dropped into the daubière to finish cooking in the "jus."

The potatoes also would take their turn in like manner, the result being that they will all receive the flavour of the gravy, and "harmonise" with the principal. Plain boiled vegetables are regarded as incomplete.

Before closing this chapter, I would mention the class of meat dishes known as the "galantines."

Although not cooked in precisely the same way, not necessarily in the daubière at all, still the principle is the same. They may be made of either cooked or uncooked meat.

When fresh meat is used, the portion is often "piqué," or larded with something which contrasts in colour, the white meat of veal has a truffle or two inserted, and red meats will have the contrast of a green nasturtium seed, etc.

I will describe the preparation of a "galantine de volaille" when made of cooked meat.

All the flesh parts of a fowl, previously boiled, should be sliced very thinly, a small quantity of ham and tongue also, a little sausage-meat mixed with chopped parsley, herbs and bread crumbs, and made up into little balls, two eggs hard boiled, also sliced, and a little red beetroot cut into strips.

Take a fluted mould, arrange these ingredients in order, having regard to the appearance when turned out, then take a cupful of clear stock, season it well, add a little gelatine (previously dissolved), colour it a light brown, and pour over all. Place the mould in a corner of the oven to cook gently for an hour, then weight it well, and stand aside till quite cold.

A galantine made of fresh meat would, of course, take longer to cook, but it would also require pressing with a weight, as these dishes are intended to be sliced very delicately.

As luncheon, supper, or "reserve" dishes they will be found exceedingly useful, looking as well as tasting very good.

CHAPTER VII.

Frying and "Sauté"-ing.

FRYING plays an important part in French cookery, but it is a very different method to that which is pursued by most English cooks.

The English way more nearly resembles what a Frenchwoman would call "to sauté," that is, to toss up, turning first to one side, then to the other, in only a little fat, while the vessel used is a shallow one.

This method has its advantages for several things—vegetables, for instance, which are to be lightly browned, chops or steaks which require very quickly doing, and most dishes of eggs, such as omelettes, although these last should have a vessel kept for their sole use.

Fish of all kinds, bread-crumbed cutlets, rissoles, fritters, etc., all require to be *plunged* into boiling fat. The principle in cooking them is the same as in boiling meat—to form a crust *at once* upon the outside that shall keep in the flavours and juices of the article fried.

For this purpose a deep iron vessel is the only true frying-pan; its depth may be from six to eight inches, and its dimensions sufficient to take in a good-sized fish. Most French pans of this description have the handles across the top, so that the pan can be hung on a chain if more convenient when using over an open fire.

Here again the charcoal stove is preferable, as the embers should be red-hot; it is impossible to fry well over a smoky or blazing fire.

These frying-pans are invariably quite half filled with fat; at first sight it may seem extravagant, but it is not really so, as with care, and taking due precautions, the same fat will serve very many times.

If poured off into a jar, which already contains a little boiling water, as soon as it is finished with, and covered over when quite cold, keeping in a cool place, it will but seldom require renewing. Of course, when fish has been fried in this, it should be reserved for that purpose alone, as also anything else of a strong flavour.

An excellent idea of good frying might be gained by watching the performance of the

"marchand de pommes-de-terre frites," whose
stall is such a common sight in the streets of
all French towns.

His little furnace is filled with coke, red-hot,
the iron pan, slung on a chain, so that he can
raise or lower it at will, is three parts full of
boiling fat. The fat he prefers, by the bye, is
suet melted, as it is clear and tasteless.

The potatoes, pared, drained, and cut into
finger lengths by a little machine made for the
purpose, are thrown into the pan, and occasionally stirred about; a few minutes see them
cooked, brown and crisp, then the pan is drawn
up, the potatoes lifted out into the strainer;
and here it should be noted how careful he is
not to leave one in the fat, lest that should, by
being overdone, impart a burnt flavour to the
rest.

In this same manner suburban Parisian
restaurants will turn out the most tempting
dishes from the rather coarse and tasteless river
fish. If the precaution is taken to have the fat
quite boiling, there is no fear of anything becoming soddened with grease when cooked in
this way. Boiling fat is generally still, free
from bubbles, and a faint blue vapour may be
seen to rise from it.

It is really more difficult to sauté to perfection than it is to fry well. In the former case, the great point to observe is to take care the sauté is not too much done, as in that case it will not be eatable. To toss it light and quickly, and remove before it has had time to become tough, is a safe rule.

Potatoes are very frequently dressed in this manner when intended to eat with veal or pork; finely chopped parsley is sprinkled over them just before serving. Cold boiled potatoes are by this means rendered equal to fresh ones.

Carrots, turnips, and parsnips, with a variety of beans, are all excellent if so treated.

Eggs may be lightly tossed in the sauté pan without actually making an omelette of them. Parsley is a great addition to all sautés.

A favourite form of using up cold meat by frying is to make " rissoles."

Remains of any meat or poultry, with a few bread-crumbs, herbs and a minced shallot, and a little good sauce to moisten the whole.

Roll out a sheet of paste (puff paste is the best) to an eighth of an inch in thickness, cut into squares, place a little of the mince in the middle, fold over securely, and fasten the edges together with white of egg: plunge into the pan of boiling fat, let them cook a few minutes, when they will swell out and become deliciously crisp and brown.

If drained on a sheet of blotting-paper, then garnished with curled parsley, quite a handsome dish may be obtained at a very small cost.

Sweet rissoles may be made the same way, substituting minced apples, bread crumbs, and a little honey for the meat.

The "Beignet aux pommes," the really genuine apple fritter, is rather different to the apple fritter of the English cook.

The batter is made by mixing a tablespoonful of flour smoothly with a little water, then adding a little salt, a spoonful of olive oil, and two beaten whites of eggs.

The apples are pared, quartered, and evenly sliced, then allowed to soak a little while in some sweet wine, with a few drops of lemon-juice. When ready to use them, dip each piece in the batter, and drop into the boiling fat. When cooked and drained, they should be liberally frosted with white sugar.

Oranges may be done in this way, also rhubarb cut into short pieces. Many little cakes made of dough may be fried in this way, and they are truly delicious.

Where butter or meat fat is difficult to obtain, boiling oil is used for the same purposes; it is an excellent substitute when once one has become accustomed to the flavour.

In Italy and Spain it is generally preferred to any other fat.

French pancakes or "crêpes" are dropped into boiling fat; hence the curious shapes they assume: the cause of much merriment at carnival parties.

But they are certainly not superior to the genuine English pancake, the shallow frying-pan being eminently suited to this dish, and here at least the English cook can hold her own.

It used to be the boast of the old race of Virginian cooks that they could toss a pancake with such accuracy up the mouth of the wide chimney, that it would turn itself, and come down, like St. Lawrence, ready to have the other side fried.

Fortunately, it is not necessary to attain the skill needful to perform this acrobatic exploit in order to turn out a first-class pancake. In the making of these, as in most other things, experience is the best teacher.

The distinction should always be observed

between a fritter and a pancake, remembering that the one is boiled in fat, while the other is fried—first one side and then the other.

When making a number of fritters or small things, it is a great convenience to place them in one of the wire baskets, sold for the purpose, before plunging them in the pan.

Omelettes are a "race apart," and will be found under the head of "Maigre Dishes." They can scarcely be said to be fried, and they certainly are not boiled.

CHAPTER VIII.

Some Gâteaux and Compotes.

WHILE standing pre-eminent in the art of pastry-making, the French cook is not great in the matter of cakes. A glance at the " Patissier's " window will show this directly. Amongst all the appetising array of dainty confections the number of cakes may be counted upon one's fingers. And the "bourgeoise ménagère" would never dream of making a loaf of cake, although she has a great appreciation of both plum-cake and plum-pudding; while her English sister is ever on the look-out for something new to add to her already lengthy list.

Here, be it stated, the "gâteau" is not exactly a "cake," it is rather a dessert dish, and as such is most generally used in the country where puddings are little known. Although some of them in their fanciful decoration are beyond the scope of the amateur, still a few of them may be fairly well imitated.

The "Génoise fourrée" is the foundation of many charming gâteaux—the fourrée, or filling, being varied at will.

The number of eggs needed depends upon the size of the gâteau required. The whites and yolks are separated, and both thoroughly beaten; with the yolks a little rose water or orange-flower water is mixed; pounded sugar and fine dry flour in proportions of a quarter of a pound of each to four eggs; the whites are added last of all, and the whole thoroughly beaten, then poured into a well-buttered tin not more than two to three inches in depth, and baked in a quick oven till a delicate brown.

For a "gâteau d'Abricots," this would be split open and apricot preserve spread between; the whole would then be covered with clear sugar icing, and richly ornamented with candied fruits. Or sometimes in place of preserve will be found the "crême Frangipane" and the icing, or, as a substitute for the icing, caramel would be used.

The same foundation is used for a chocolate or coffee cream gâteau; the cream consisting of butter and pounded sugar well beaten together, with the addition of made coffee or chocolate. This being very stiff is used also for the outside decoration, and is wreathed into many fantastic forms; the outer edge of the gâteau being covered with grated almonds.

"Pâté d'Eclair" is the foundation of quite a distinct kind of gâteau.

Its ingredients are butter, flour, and beaten eggs, no sugar, but a pinch of salt. The butter is first dissolved in a lined saucepan, the flour briskly stirred in, a small quantity of warm milk added, and this is boiled, stirring rapidly all the time, for about five minutes. It must not be stiff even then, therefore but a small quantity of flour is needed. Let this become cool before stirring into it the well-whisked eggs.

For "Eclairs aux Chocolat" this batter would be poured into little boat-shaped moulds, well oiled, and when cooked they would be split open and a spoonful of custard cream inserted in the hollow, closed up again, and the outside coated over with melted chocolate.

"Choux à la crème" are round tartlets made of this batter, the hollow filled with cream. The pâté, if made a little stiffer, is used for fancy erections, basket-work devices, etc.

"Frangipane" is a delicious creamy custard. To beaten eggs, new milk and a very little flour are added, with fine white sugar; these are brought nearly to boiling-point, and when thick, crushed ratifias, a glass of brandy, lemon-juice, and a little butter are stirred in. Tartlets made of pâté feuilleté are filled with this.

A "gâteau au riz" is a sweet dish very popular in France. Whole rice is cooked in milk till quite soft, and the milk nearly absorbed; then sugar, lemon-juice, a little butter, and beaten eggs are well stirred in. The mixture is poured into a shallow mould, which has been well buttered and coated with fine bread-crumbs and sugar. This is baked until firmly set, when it is turned out, and covered all over with caramel, and ornamented according to fancy. It is always eaten cold.

The "brioche" is quite a different production to the English bun. One-third of the quantity of flour intended to be used is mixed to a very soft paste with a little frothing yeast and warm water; with the other two-thirds of flour, eggs, a little butter, a few currants, salt, and more warm water are mixed to a soft paste again. These two pastes are then kneaded together to form a dough, which is left to rise several hours; then the brioches are cut out, brushed over with egg and milk, and baked very quickly. They are exceedingly light, and much liked by people who do not care for sweet cakes.

The same mixture is baked in loaves, which are cut up and buttered, as for bread and butter.

The cakes made at the fêtes in the country towns and villages are very similar, more or less rich, with or without the fruit, according to the custom of the district.

Here should be mentioned the " tarte," the genuine country tart, which makes its appearance on every table when the " ducasse" or " wakes" come round. The crust bears some resemblance to the " pâté d'Eclair," but the country flour renders it much more substantial ; the custard which frills it is a wonderful compound of eggs, milk and sugar, spice, with here and there an occasional raisin making its appearance.

When well made, this compound is very good, but an inferior make has an unfortunate resemblance to leather, and needs a country appetite to make it " go down."

When making tarts of fresh fruit, the " bourgeoise " will invariably make a marmalade of her fruit before laying it on her crust; placing a lattice-work of strips of pastry to finish off the top. A fruit " pie," or tart, with the crust over the fruit, is quite unknown in France.

Puddings are but little adopted in French families, gaufres and biscuits, with " confiture," in winter, or compote of fruit in summer. Fresh fruit and cheese is the general finish to a dinner.

Pastry and sweets are only indulged in on Sundays and extra occasions.

Nearly all fruits may be made into compotes. The syrup should be made first by dissolving sugar in water, and allowing it to boil; then the fruit is added, whole or divided, and cooked until tender; the syrup remaining after the fruit is removed may be boiled till it thickens, and receive colouring to make it contrast, if desired.

A compote of apples, pared and quartered, cooked in clear syrup, the remaining liquor coloured with cochineal, makes a very pretty dish. Pears invariably receive the addition of claret, and they are cooked in the oven, as they require a much longer time. The wine is thought no extravagance, as it so greatly enriches the fruit.

There is a very wide difference between a compote and "stewed fruit," but with the former, as with the latter, the addition of a little whipped cream or custard is a great improvement.

The good "ménagère" generally prefers to make her own "liqueurs." For all of them the fruit is steeped in spirit till all the goodness is extracted, then sugar equal to the weight of the liquor is added, and all boiled together for about twenty minutes. When cool, it is bottled off. They make very wholesome drinks with the addition of water.

There is a sweet pickle of very high repute in Switzerland. Date-plums, dry and sound, and not too ripe, are taken and placed in salt and water for forty-eight hours. They are then drained and dried in the sun. Afterwards they are put into jars, and boiling vinegar with pounded sugar (a pound to a pint) is poured over them. When cool, they are closely covered and set away. It is a delicious pickle for cold meat. Cherries also are very good done this way.

Soufflé un Citron.

A soufflé may be either steamed or baked; in either case it must be eaten without a moment's loss of time, as it falls directly. Remember also to only partly fill the mould which is used; this species of "gâteau" usually trebles itself in size while cooking.

To make a soufflé for six persons, take a pint of milk, four ounces of lump sugar, and three fresh eggs. Boil the milk and sugar, together with the pared lemon rind, in a lined saucepan. Mix smoothly with a little cold milk, two table- spoonfuls of flour, then pour the boiling milk on to this, taking care there are no lumps. Return all to the saucepan, and boil, stirring rapidly, for three or four minutes, then pour this into a basin.

When the above mixture is perfectly cold, beat into it the whisked yolks of eggs, the juice of half a lemon (the rind must have been re- moved before), and lastly the frothed whites. Have your mould well buttered, pour the mix- ture into it, and either bake or steam it (without a cover) for twenty minutes. The cover of the steamer must of course be fastened down; there should be sufficient depth of pan to allow of the soufflé rising without coming in contact with the lid. Serve *citron sauce* with this soufflé. (*See* Chapter V.)

If preferred, the flavouring may be omitted from the soufflé, and a chocolate sauce made and poured round it on the dish. For the latter, scrape or dissolve a tablet of chocolate, add a quarter of a pint of water to it, and a teaspoonful of cornflour to give smoothness and substance; boil well.

It will be easily seen that a plain soufflé may

be varied by the admixture of almost any flavouring, also by the variety of sauces served with it.

The first part of the mixture may be made any time in advance.

Diplomate.

Remove the crust from some thin slices of stale white bread, and stamp them into small rounds; dip each one in sweet wine. (If preferred, sponge biscuits or stale sponge cakes may be used instead.) Butter a plain round mould. Arrange the rounds evenly at the bottom and sides, sprinkle the bottom with stoned raisins, a few currants and strips of candied peel. Put another layer of bread or biscuits next, and alternate thus with the fruit until the mould is three-quarters filled. Boil a pint of milk, pour it after sweetening upon two beaten eggs, add spice and salt; then carefully pour this custard into the mould. Let the mould stand for two or three hours, then bake or steam it for three-quarters to one hour. Turn out, and serve with wine or custard sauce poured round it.

Savarin.

The mould generally used for this is a large ring with a hollow centre.

The ingredients required are half a pound of fine flour, a quarter of a pound of butter, half a tumblerful of warm milk, an ounce of fresh German yeast, a tablespoonful of sugar and half a teaspoonful of salt, with two eggs.

Put the flour in a basin, make a hollow in the centre, and put in the yeast mixed smoothly with warm water and the milk; mix this with sufficient of the flour to make a stiff dough. Cover the basin, and set that in a warm place where the sponge may rise. When it has risen to twice its original size, add to it the sugar, the butter ready dissolved (but not too warm), salt, and the eggs—broken but not beaten. Knead these all briskly together with the hand, until the dough appears all bubbles.

Butter the mould, and sprinkle the inside with blanched and chopped almonds and powdered sugar. Half fill it with the paste; set in a warm place to rise until the mould becomes quite full.

Bake it in a quick oven for about half an hour. Let it slightly cool, then turn out on to

a fancy dish, and pour over it the following
syrup :—

Four ounces of sugar boiled with a tumblerful of water, and flavoured with a little rum or
essence.

Galette Cherbourgeoise.

Dissolve a quarter of a pound of butter, and
work it into half a pound of baker's dough ;
add to it two beaten eggs, two spoonfuls of
spirits of wine or other spirit, and half a teaspoonful of salt.   Knead or beat well for several
minutes ; let it stand in a warm place to rise
for a couple of hours, place in a buttered tin
which it will only three parts fill, and bake for
thirty minutes ; turn out and serve hot.

Galette Lorraine.

Rub together half a pound of flour and half
as much butter, add a pinch of salt and an egg,
with water sufficient to form a stiff paste.
Roll out to the thickness of a five-shilling piece,
place on a buttered tin, crimp the edge, then
bake in the oven for a few minutes ; when
partly done draw it out, and pour upon it a
cream made from two beaten eggs and a cup of
sweetened milk.   Sprinkle a few chopped nuts

over, and bake until the custard is set and browned.

Saint Honoré.

Make a paste by putting into a saucepan a tumblerful of water, a little sugar, the size of an egg in butter, a pinch of salt, and a small bit of lemon rind; and when these are boiling, dredge lightly and carefully in with one hand (stirring vigorously all the time with the other) sufficient flour to make a light paste.

Keep stirring for five minutes longer, then take off the fire, and allow the paste to cool. When cool, break into it three eggs, one after the other, beating the paste all the time.

Form part of this paste as the crust of a tart-let, and bake it in the oven till of a bright brown.

Drop the remaining paste in small balls on to a buttered tin; bake them also. When the tartlet is done, take these balls, coat them with melted sugar, and place them all round the edge of it, pour the remaining syrup over all the edge again. Fill the interior with a thick pastry cream, or whipped cream, and serve fresh.

Marasquin.

Blanch and crush half a pound of sweet almonds. Add to the paste four ounces of

butter or pure lard, four ounces of dry flour,
the same weight of sugar, two eggs—the whites
and yolks beaten separately, two spoonfuls of
orange-flower water, a pinch of salt and spoonful
of cream.

Beat these ingredients well together, and
spread them over a round of good puff paste.
Bake for upwards of half an hour. Glaze the
surface with sugar and water, or a little dissolved sweet jelly.

Quatre-quarts.   (*Four Quarters.*)

Take three or four eggs. The same weight
in flour, butter, and powdered sugar; mix all
well together, and add a glassful of spirit or
orange flower-water to the whole. The whites
of the eggs should be beaten stiff and added
lastly. Butter a mould, sugar it well, and bake
the cake in a moderate oven for upwards of an
hour.

May be flavoured at discretion.

Gâteau d'œufs, au Vanille.

Separate the yolks and whites of four eggs.
Beat the whites to a stiff froth, then lightly stir
into them four spoonfuls of powdered sugar
and a few drops of essence of vanilla (if vanilla

is disliked, use lemon-juice) ; have ready a fancy mould well buttered and sprinkled inside with sugar. Pour the whites into this—they should not more than half fill it—and steam the mould, setting it in a *bain-marie*. When it has well risen and seems set, turn it out on to a dish, and pour round it a sweet custard made from the yolks. Garnish with currant jelly.

Crème Renversée.

For a moderately large mould take a quart of milk and boil it with half a pound of lump sugar and fresh lemon rind, or part of a pod of vanilla. When cooled a little, stir it into eight eggs lightly beaten, the yolks and whites together, then pour this cream into a buttered mould which will just contain it, and set the mould in a *bain-marie* or in a cool oven. When the cream is become solid, set the mould in a cold place, and when required turn it out on to a dish, and place currant jelly around it.

Crème Sambayone.

Separate the yolks and whites of six eggs. Place the yolks in a saucepan, with three table-spoonfuls of sugar and a wineglassful of rum or brandy ; stir these briskly together over the fire

until the mixture begins to thicken, when with-
draw it at once. Beat the whites to a stiff froth
and stir them into the yolks when the latter
mixture is cool. Pour into small glasses or
cups.

Charlotte Russe.

Line the bottom and sides of a plain mould
with finger biscuits and ratafias. Fill up the
mould with whipped cream, or a cream made
with isinglass, which when cold will become
solid.

Set the mould on ice or in a very cold place.
Turn out of the mould just before bringing to
the table.

Compote of Quinces.

Throw some quinces into boiling water for a
few minutes, lift them out and pour a little cold
water over them. Next, peel them carefully,
take out seeds and cores, quarter and sub-
quarter them and put these latter into a little
clear boiling syrup and allow them to cook until
thoroughly done. Take the fruit out on to a
dish, boil the syrup a little longer to reduce it,
then pour over the fruit.

Compote of Pears.

Pare the pears very thinly, slice them not too thinly, but removing the pips. Lay them in a stewpan with two or three lumps of sugar, a clove or two, and blade of cinnamon. Pour over them a tumblerful of claret and water enough to just cover them. Cover up the stewpan, place it in the corner of the oven and let the pears cook gently thus for at least an hour or more.

Compote of Cherries.

Make a clear syrup with sugar and a little water. Cut away all the stalk save about half an inch from some sour cherries. Let them cook in the syrup until thoroughly soft. Allow them to get cold in this before removing them to a dish.

Compote of Plums.

Make the syrup, and put the plums in when it is boiling hot. Let them cook not too rapidly, until they show signs of breaking, then remove them to a dish, and pour the syrup over.

Compote of Prunes.

Let the prunes soak for several hours in cold water. Pour away this water, then place the prunes in a stewpan with sufficient fresh water to cover them and a few lumps of sugar. Cover closely and cook slowly for a couple of hours.

Compote of Rhubarb.

Make a little syrup; cut the rhubarb—after wiping with a clean cloth—into inch lengths. Drop the pieces into the syrup and cook until they show signs of breaking. Remove the fruit to a dish. Add a few drops of lemon juice to the syrup, boil it until it becomes reduced, and pour over the rhubarb.

When making a compote of strawberries use red currant juice instead of water for the syrup.

It is generally sufficient to pour a boiling syrup *over* ripe strawberries, having the berries in a dish which will not break, and letting them lie in the syrup until perfectly cold before removing to their proper dish.

CHAPTER IX.

"Maigre" Dishes.

WHILE, in the present degenerate days, "fast days" are but little observed in comparison with the fashion of keeping them in the old times, when the "curés" held undisputed sway, still, amongst fairly good Catholics, Friday is set apart as a day when no meat shall appear on the table—while the weeks of Lent are the butcher's holiday time.

Good Friday is rigidly kept as a day of abstinence by all classes; almost superstitiously kept, indeed, for to eat meat or any animal fat on that day would be regarded as a wilful courting of calamity. Even eggs and butter are excluded from the menu of the good Catholic on that occasion.

As a rule, to "faire maigre" is merely to abstain from meat, its place being taken by fish. During the Lenten season it is somewhat

106

difficult to find vegetables to make separate dishes from, the winter's supply being nearly exhausted, or becoming tough, while it is still too early in the year to look for fresh ones.

The "ménagère," therefore, looks to her fowl pen as her great resource, and, fortunately, eggs are by then both good and plentiful and fairly cheap. Fish is generally abundant at that time, and a good choice to be had.

Almost all vegetable soups come under the title of "maigre," but "potage au lait" is eminently entitled to do so. In the best "cuisines" it is made after this fashion.

A quart of milk is boiled for a little time to extract the flavour from a small piece of lemon rind, a few coriander seeds, and a small piece of stick cinnamon ; a pinch of salt and several lumps of sugar. It is then strained, and a small quantity poured over the soft part of a thick slice of bread cut into dice, and put in the tureen.

This is placed where it will keep hot, and into the remainder of the milk two yolks of eggs should be stirred, and then allowed to boil till they slightly thicken the milk, when it also is poured into the tureen and served immediately.

"Bisque," made from crab, is generally thought to be a rather rare dish, but it can be made with very little trouble.

From a cooked crab all the fleshy part should be taken and carefully pounded in a mortar with an equal quantity of boiled rice, a little water, and cayenne pepper; pass it through a tamis, and add a sufficient quantity of boiling milk or cream; then pour into a hot tureen.

A very small quantity of lobster butter (which is simply the coral of a lobster pounded with butter), if stirred in, will turn it a bright red, and make a very pretty dish.

A very delicate and tasty dish of salted cod-fish is made as follows: To clear the fish from salt it is allowed to lie in water for twenty-four hours; it is then slightly boiled, drained, and broken into flakes.

Into the sauté pan a few knobs of butter are put to melt, then a little white bread, roughly crumbed, and a teacupful of cold mashed potatoes; these are tossed about with a fork, and a cupful of milk added by degrees, with a good seasoning of pepper; lastly, the flakes of cod are added, and all well beaten with the fork until it froths; it is then poured out into a hot dish and eaten with strips of toasted bread.

A favourite way of cooking flat fish, such as soles or plaice, with French cooks is to do them "au gratin." When so cooked, they should be served in the same dish; a silver one is best, but a bright block tin will answer the purpose.

The bottom of the dish is well buttered, and spread with finely-minced herbs, a shallot or two, seasoning, and bread-crumbs. The fish is placed upon this bed, and covered over with the same mixture; then placed in the oven to bake. A glass of white wine is generally added.

"Sole à la Normande" is done similarly to the preceding; but a rich sauce, made of melted butter, yolks of eggs, button mushrooms, oysters, and a little lemon-juice and white wine, is poured over the fish before sending to table. It is a truly Epicurean dish.

Mackerel and herrings are excellent when split open, boned, and broiled over a clear fire; they are better still if the following sauce be poured over them: Melted butter (slightly thickened with flour), a spoonful of vinegar, the same of Worcestershire sauce, also one of chopped parsley; pepper and salt to taste.

We will now consider the subject of omelettes —one of the easiest things to make, and also

one of the easiest to spoil. It is strange how
few English cooks seem able to turn out a
really good omelette, and yet the veriest "pay-
sanne" in a country café in sunny France will
make one, at a moment's notice, to satisfy the
most critical taste.

Let us, in imagination, visit one of these
cafés, and watch how the good wife proceeds.
Setting a light to her charcoal braisière, she
will wait till the embers are red, then put on
her pan, generally a black iron sauté pan, kept
for this purpose alone; into this she drops a
lump of butter, and while it is melting she
breaks her eggs on to a plate, beats them
quickly with a knife, and adds salt and pepper
to them.

When the butter is frothing and turning
brown, she pours in the eggs, slips a knife
underneath the middle and round the edge, to
insure it not sticking to the pan, and as soon as
ever it is "set," she "whips" off her pan,
claps a hot plate over it, and with a dexterous
twist manages to turn it upside down, and remove the pan, leaving the omelette on the plate
—light, with a delicate brown crust uppermost.

This plain omelette may be varied *ad in-*

finitum by adding minced onion, herbs, parsley, mushrooms, cheese, or whatever fancy may dictate.

Another way of making omelettes is to beat the eggs, whites and yolks separately, and add a few spoonfuls of milk. This makes quite a different kind, and is more suitable for sweet omelettes when preserves or jellies are eaten with them.

Two eggs per person is a very moderate allowance when making single omelettes. When several persons are intending to partake at the same time, it is better to use more eggs, and make one large one.

Salad is a delicious companion dish to a savoury omelette, and makes it a very substantial luncheon or supper dish. When ham is obtainable, some very thin slices slightly frizzled are also an excellent addition, when not intending to make a meal exclusively "au maigre."

Eggs are also very good when cooked "au gratin." The same preparation is used as for "sole au gratin," and the eggs broken on to the bed, and allowed to cook until just firm.

A great variety of excellent "maigre" dishes may be made from rice and macaroni. Rice is, perhaps, most generally liked when used for sweet dishes, or in curries. With cheese or fruit it is an excellent food.

Macaroni is not generally appreciated in England, but on the Continent it becomes a wholesome and delicious preparation. Dishes of macaroni, with tomatoes, mushrooms, truffles, cheese, or fish are all good.

The following recipe may be novel to many people :—After the macaroni has been boiled and drained, put it into a stewpan with a lump of butter, two tablespoonfuls of cream, and as much grated Parmesan as will make it as thick as custard; toss well together with a fork; then take a French roll, which has been previously soaked in wine and made hot; pour the macaroni over it, and slightly brown in the oven.

Always put macaroni into boiling water with salt; allow twenty minutes for it to cook through; then drain well before using it.

As being pre-eminently Lenten faring, most of the recipes for the cooking of fish will be found grouped under this heading.

The method of cooking fish "au gratin" has been detailed above; the following is another capital way of treating flat fish :—

After washing and drying, cut it down the middle on the white side, carefully raise the meat from the bones on each side, but do not lift it right off. Prepare a little light, well-seasoned stuffing of bread-crumbs, parsley, butter-seasoning and egg, no milk; spread this on the under side of the raised flesh, press it down to the bone again, brush over the surface with beaten egg, sprinkle with seasoned crumbs; lay the fish in a buttered tin, put dabs of butter over the top, and bake for about fifteen minutes in a quick oven. The fish should be well browned on the surface, then slipped out on to a hot dish, and a white or brown sauce, with capers or chopped gherkins, poured around—not over—it.

Morue à la Hollandaise.

A cod's head and shoulders or a whole fish is best served this way.

Boiled in water containing plenty of salt and one or two lemons cut in quarters. Drain it when a skewer will penetrate to the bone with ease. Lay on a folded serviette, place large, mealy, boiled potatoes around it, and tufts of curly parsley. Send pure butter melted to table in a tureen.

Baked Cod.

A fair-sized piece out of the middle of a cod. Crimp it, by cutting it through to the bone at regular distances. Sprinkle it liberally, inside and out, with pepper and salt and fresh parsley, squeeze lemon juice over it, lay in a baking tin, and bake in moderate oven, with frequent bastings of butter. Serve with "maître-d'hôtel" butter.

Halibut Steaks

may be baked "au gratin," or grilled, or fried, and served with a brown "sauce piquante," or they may be done

à la Crème.

Dissolve an ounce of butter, stir into it a tablespoonful of flour, a little salt and pepper, and add a tumblerful of hot water. Lay the halibut in a buttered shallow stewpan, cover it with this sauce, let it simmer gently (covered over) until tender. A small white onion and bunch of sweet herbs should be put in the pan at the same time. When the fish is sufficiently cooked remove it to a dish and keep hot.

Take out the onion and flavourings, and

thicken the sauce by adding the yolk of an egg
and a few spoonfuls of cream to it; then pour
it over the fish. A hard-boiled egg cut up small
should be sprinkled over the top of all; or,
instead of adding yolk of egg to the sauce, stir
in a spoonful of anchovy essence with the cream,
and use lobster coral, picked shrimps or prawns
for the surface decoration.

Salmon Steaks,

wrapped in buttered notepaper, and slowly
grilled over a clear, hot, but not blazing fire,
then eaten with *"petits pois"* (see sequel to
Chapter III.) are an Epicurean dish.

Red mullet enveloped in the same manner—
not stinting the butter, by the way—may be
either baked or grilled, and are most delicious.

When a portion out of the middle of a salmon
is the piece chosen, it will be found that *baking*
it is a method preferable to the *boiling* thereof;
although no method can surpass boiling for this
king of fish if it be a whole one or a very large
piece.

Squeeze a little fresh lemon juice over it
before baking, and use only the best fresh
butter.

Mackerel and Herrings,

like most oily fish, will be found to bake better
than boil. When possible the bones should be
removed, the fish rubbed on both sides with
lemon juice, some fresh minced herbs and seasoning, with a few bread-crumbs, laid on the flat
inner side of one fish, another one being laid
sandwich fashion over this, then both baked together, using but a very tiny bit of butter, only
sufficient to keep the fish from adhering to the
tin.

There are two ways of *pickling* fish—*i.e.*, for
the lighter and more delicate kinds, taking the
remaining portions of the fish after boiling, lay
the meat flakes in a china dish, season lightly,
place a few leaves of fennel, tarragon or parsley
about, and pour a little white wine vinegar over
all. Set aside until required.

Pickled mackerel, herrings, etc., after very
thorough washing are laid in a pie-dish,
sprinkled with salt, several pepper-corns added,
and vinegar sufficient to cover them. Baked
until they show signs of leaving the bone.

In boiling any kind of fish it is better to have
the water very nearly at boiling point when the

fish is put in, to bring it to the boil as quickly as possible, then to draw the pan aside and *simmer* until done.

Never cook fish until it will not keep its shape ; as soon as a fine skewer will penetrate its thickest part it is done.

For using up the remains of fish—when there are any nice pieces—few methods are better than to curry it. The flakes of fish will, however, only require to be made hot in the curry, not cooked in it.

A little vegetable or fruit—apple, rhubarb or gooseberry,—are needed in a fish curry, and eggs boiled hard and sliced, or boiled rice for its garnish.

A Mayonnaise

of cold boiled or baked fish is another excellent and delicate way of using up the remains.

A crisp white-hearted lettuce, the fish broken into small flakes, sliced or chopped boiled egg, and a little good mayonnaise sauce (see Chapter V.) poured over all, and prettily decorated.

We have it on the authority of Professor Matthieu Williams that the chief reason why cheese is found to be difficult of digestion is because the mineral properties of the milk have been left behind in the whey. To neutralise the acid remaining in cheese, and to supply the deficiency mentioned, he advocates the use of a very small quantity of bicarbonate of potash— a proportion of a quarter of an ounce to every pound of cheese. This addition may be made to almost any dish in cheese cookery, and in this proportion will never be detected.

The experiment is well worth the attention of those who, liking cheese, are yet unable to assimilate it.

Cheese Pudding,

baked or steamed.

Butter a small pudding mould, half fill it with thin slices of stale bread and butter—no crust— and between each slice make a layer of grated cheese. One beaten egg, half a small teaspoonful of mixed salt and pepper, and enough warm milk to fill the mould, mixed together, a pinch of bicarbonate of potash being stirred into this, then the mould filled up. Cover with a plate, and let the pudding stand for at least an hour before cooking it. Bake in gentle oven for half an hour, steam for three-quarters.

Cheese Fondu.

Equal quantities of bread-crumbs and grated cheese, a little salt and pinch of cayenne, a small nob of butter melted, one or two beaten eggs, and milk to make it of the consistency of cream. Bake in shallow buttered dish till crisp and brown.

Cheese Darioles.

Make some dariole shapes from good short paste, fill up with the following mixture, and bake in a quick oven till browned. Yolks of two eggs, white of one, a spoonful of melted butter or cream, two spoonfuls of grated cheese, pinch of potash, pepper and salt, mix together.

Savoury Baked Rice.

Cree a cupful of whole rice until tender, mix with it half a pint of milk, a beaten egg, pinch of cayenne, and a little salt, and some stale grated cheese of good flavour. Bake this mixture until well set in a buttered mould; when done, turn it on to a dish, and surround it with a brown "sauce piquante," or a tomato purée sharply seasoned. Or it may be served cold with a nicely dressed salad.

Cheese Fricassée.

Frizzle a sliced Spanish onion in a little butter; when brown, add to it a tablespoonful of brown *roux* or other brown sauce, sufficient warm water to make it of the right consistency; season it well. Slice into this some stale Stilton, Cheddar, or other cheese, and let it gradually become very hot, but beware of allowing it to boil. Serve very hot, with toast "fingers" or with boiled cauliflower.

Cheese Sandwiches.

Cut some thin slices of bread and butter, brown or white; cut off all crust. Spread grated cheese plentifully between, and pepper them well. Cut into small squares, and garnish with fresh watercress or parsley.

Very nice for luncheon or supper, with celery or watercress.

Another way:

Spread cream cheese over the bread in lieu of butter; sprinkle with chopped cress, pepper lightly, and dust with salt.

Cream Cheese Salads.

Prepare a little dressing first of all by mincing together a small shallot, sprigs of chervil, thyme, parsley, tarragon, etc., and adding to them a pinch of salt and pepper, with a tablespoonful of lemon juice and three of salad oil; then mix all well together. Separate the leaves of a crisp, well-hearted lettuce; in the hollow of each leaf place a little rocky lump of cream cheese. Pour a spoonful of the dressing over, then arrange the leaves singly on a dish. Garnish with red radishes.

Cheese Omelette.

Break four eggs on to a plate, add to them a pinch of salt and pepper, and a spoonful of grated cheese; beat up with the blade of a knife. Pour the mixture into the omelette pan, which should contain plenty of frothing butter. Stir it once or twice, when it is set sufficiently, fold one half over, slip it out on to a dish, grate a little more cheese on the top, and serve very hot. If not too stale, the cheese may be sliced, instead of grated.

Mushroom Omelette.

Remove the skins and stalks from half a dozen mushrooms; cut them small, add a minced shallot and teaspoonful of parsley, pepper and salt, then cook these together in a little butter.

Make a plain omelette, lay the cooked mushrooms on the one half, and fold over.

Onion Omelette.

Slice very thinly, and frizzle with the butter in the omelette pan, two small white onions. When they are brown, pour in the beaten eggs and seasoning, and cook as usual. Sprinkle the surface with a little parsley before bringing to table.

Au Fines Herbes.

Beat the eggs as for plain omelettes, and stir into them chopped chives, parsley, chervil, or any herb available. Season and cook as before directed.

Omelette au Sucre.

Beat the yolks separately in one basin, the whites in another; to the yolks add a tablespoonful of powdered sugar, pinch of salt, and one or two spoonfuls of milk ; stir in the whites, and pour into the frothing butter. When the mixture is set, fold it over, sprinkling powdered sugar over the top.

Omelette au Rhum.

Make a sweet omelette as above ; sugar it freely, and pour a wineglassful of rum or brandy around it, setting fire to the latter before bringing to table.

Oeufs à la Neige.

Boil a pint of milk with a pinch of salt, a few lumps of sugar, and small piece of fresh lemon rind. When it boils remove the rind, and having ready the whites of two or three eggs beaten to a stiff froth, take up the latter by tablespoonfuls, drop them carefully in the milk, and poach them thus for a few moments. Lift each " snowball " out on to a dish, and when all are done pour the beaten yolks into the remainder of the milk, and stir until a thickish custard is formed. When the custard is cool, pour it round the snowballs in the dish, and sprinkle a few candied cherries about.

A very pretty dish.

Timbale of Macaroni.

Line a round mould with good short paste; fill it with the following preparation, and put on the cover, closing the edges with beaten egg, and bake for three-quarters of an hour in moderate oven. Slip it carefully out of the mould, so as not to disturb the shape. Serve hot.

Filling: Make a "sauce financière" (see Chapter V.), and stir into it a quarter of a pound of cooked macaroni.

Or a white sauce may be made instead, the macaroni added, also some grated cheese.

CHAPTER X.

Fricassées and Rechauffées.

WITHOUT actually coming within the range of what may be called "fried" dishes—that is, such as have been treated of under the heading of the "Frying-pan"—there are sometimes occasions arising in the good ménagère's arrangements for her table when she finds it wise to imitate somewhat the example of "good King Arthur's" economical spouse, and "what they could not eat that day, next day fry," by warming up in a delicate fashion, akin to frying, it is true, and yet with a degree of difference.

A fricassée *par excellence* generally means fricassée of chicken, one which has been partially cooked expressly to be used in this manner; but although poultry is especially nice, other meats may be made into very savoury dishes in the same way. Many puddings will also lend themselves to this sort of "warming up."

Poultry should be cut up into small joints, and all meat is better if small thick pieces are made of it for a fricassée ; a sauce or batter is then made as follows : all trimmings and portions not nice enough for the dish are boiled in a little stock with one or two onions, and a few herbs ; the fat removed. It is then thickened with a yolk of egg mixed with a little flour. Each piece of chicken or meat is dipped in this, and then well crumbed over, and carefully fried.

The remainder of the sauce may be browned, a spoonful of good ketchup added, then poured round the dish of crisp, brown morsels. Some French cooks would fry the pieces in oil seasoned with garlic, but the above method is more generally practised. Of course this is a superior fricassée.

For an ordinary family dish a plain batter would do, taking care to crumb over the pieces after they had been dipped in it; and if a few vegetables, such as carrots and parsnips, with small onions, are also fried until just tender and lightly browned, then put with the bits of meat and a little gravy poured round, a very

appetising dish may be obtained at a little cost.
The potatoes which accompany this should also
be fried.

Another nice way, supposing the ménagère
has some cold lean beef—not too much cooked
—which requires warming up, is to cut it into
thin strips and slice some bacon very thinly,
laying beef and bacon together; roll them up,
fastening with a tiny skewer, and then dip in
batter and fry them. A "sauce piquante"
should be served with the rolls.

Then, again, meat may be cut into dice, with
a little fat bacon, a little cooked vegetable, and
chopped onion, and fried in some hot fat in
the sauté pan. Let this be lightly tossed about
until just brown, remove all superfluous fat and
dredge a little flour over all; a cupful of stock
liquor should be poured in and the sauté pan
drawn away from the fire, leaving it to cook
gently while you make a potato crust, either of
cold mashed potatoes or freshly cooked ones.
Mix them with an egg and a little milk to make
them smooth, then cover a shallow tin plate
about half an inch thick with this crust, crimp
the edges and bake until brown, when the contents of the sauté pan should be poured into
the middle.

Meat, particularly beef and veal, may be "réchauffé" by making a good thick gravy or sauce and laying in it the meat, cut in thin slices, to simmer gently till hot through without cooking it again. If ham or bacon be added in this case it should be frizzled first, then put on the top when the dish is served.

Mutton is better made into a ragoût. For this a deep pie dish will answer the purpose excellently well—or the daubière. Potatoes and onions pared and sliced evenly, the mutton (generally cooked) also sliced and each piece dipped into flour; fill the dish with alternate layers of these, then pour over some stock liquor made from bones, and a liberal seasoning of salt and pepper; the dish is then well covered over and put in the oven for an hour and a half.

If fresh mutton is used for a ragoût, portions of the breast and trimmings will make the dish quite well enough.

Another way of making a ragoût is to cut the fresh meat into equal sized pieces, flour each one, cut a little salt bacon into strips, and a variety of vegetables also, arranging these ingredients in layers in a covered stewpan, and dredging flour between with salt and pepper; then cover with water and leave to cook gently in a corner of the oven for some time—about a couple of hours.

A *fricandeau* is similar to the above, only the meat would be left in one piece—a short thick piece is to be preferred, and if lean it may be larded. A slice of fat pork or bacon should cover the bottom of the stewpan; any vegetables may be used for this, and they should be placed around the piece of meat and over it. A cupful of stock poured over all.

When cooked the meat and vegetables should be lifted on to a dish, the gravy skimmed from all fat, and a little thickening and seasoning added; it should then be allowed to boil a few minutes before pouring over the dish.

Nearly all fricandeaux are made after this fashion; salsify, chicory or sorrel, and spinach, are good vegetables to use for this dish.

Curries are well known in England, but the preparations known as "à la financière" may be somewhat novel.

Various small things go to the composition of a financière sauce—mushrooms, quenelles, cockscombs, sweetbreads sliced, sometimes truffles, giblets, etc.; these are slowly cooked in a rich brown sauce, and a glass of good wine.

This is chiefly used in garnishing entrées and other dishes. Quenelles are small balls made of delicate forcemeat.

A veal cutlet "à la financière" is cooked as follows: the cutlet is boned, and the lean part larded through with strips of bacon.

The bottom of a small stewpan is lined with a slice of bacon, sliced carrot, onion, celery, and a bunch of herbs. The cutlet is laid upon these, and sufficient stock poured over to barely touch the meat; it is then covered with a greased paper, and stewed gently until the cutlet is quite tender.

After lifting out, the gravy is strained, the vegetable crushed into a purée, thickened and browned, a glass of sherry is added, and a good pinch of cayenne, some ketchup and seasoning. This is poured round the cutlet, and served very hot.

Sweetbreads are very nice, done exactly the same way; always, of course, parboiling them first.

An excellent and cheap way to *réchauffer* a very small remainder of cold meat is to mince it finely, add bread-crumbs and a little piquante sauce or gravy sufficient to moisten well. A small vegetable marrow is pared, and the inside emptied, and then stuffed with the above mince, a little fat poured over, and then baked in the oven. A large turnip may be used in the same way when marrows are out of season.

CHAPTER XI.

Some little used Vegetables.

THERE are some few vegetables having a very extensive use in continental households, which are scarcely ever, if at all, used in England. Yet they are just as easy to cultivate as any other, and have just as valuable hygienic properties. First among them we must place *Sorrel*.

Except among the enlightened few who can boast a patch in their own garden, it is almost unknown, and, save at Covent Garden, is scarcely ever seen on the market. On the Continent it is cultivated in quantities; no little cottage garden but has its sorrel-bed, and summer or winter it appears on the table in various forms—as a soup, or a purée to eat with meat, or a sauce—and it is frequently mixed with its sister plant, the spinach, when making a vegetable dish.

Quite lately, when seeking for some in London for use at a demonstration, nothing less than a "strike" could be had, and from the Central Market only—at least ten times as much as the quantity required.

The wild sorrel which one meets with in the country is not a bad substitute, but the flavour of the cultivated kind is so superior, every garden ought to possess a few plants.

It is sown in drills like spinach; but once established, will come up year after year with faithful regularity, and if cut down every few weeks will yield several cuttings during the season.

It may also take rank as one of Nature's medicines, and help to lessen the doctor's bills, being an anti-scorbutic, simple and effective, an excellent blood-purifier, especially in spring-time.

Full directions for making sorrel soup are to be found at the end of this chapter; but here it may be well to mention that the only ingredients are sorrel and a couple of young onions, white bread, water, butter, and the *yolk* of an egg. The egg corrects the acidity of the sorrel, the bread gives substance to the soup, and the butter smoothness. As very little liquid is needed in which to cook sorrel, it is better, when intending to make a purée to serve with meat, to use a little butter in place of water. When thoroughly cooked, the sorrel should be lightly beaten with a wooden spoon, well-seasoned; then it is ready to serve either in the middle of the dish or to hand round with it.

A few leaves of sorrel, lightly chopped, give piquancy to a salad. A few leaves of sorrel may also be added to other vegetable soups, but never when there is any meat in the pot, as their acidity will tend to harden it.

Leaving the sorrel, let us consider its sister, spinach. Although we have no fault to find either with the growth or the supply of spinach, still it is in only a few better-class houses that one ever meets with the dainty dishes of spinach which are its common forms of presentation on continental tables.

It is of all green vegetables the most deceptive, shrinking to but a fraction of its original bulk when cooked.

It is also one of the dirtiest and grittiest of vegetables, and needs washing in several waters. Let it drain thoroughly, and pick out all stalky pieces. Our French friends go farther than this : they think it not too much trouble to *shred* each leaf. Staying once at a country hotel in France, we were much amused and interested to watch the old grandmother, as she sat in her chair, doing nothing else all day but prepare the vegetables for the table or the kitchen. Verily, we decided, it needed the patience of old age to prepare spinach as she did it ; but truly, when it came to table, it was as nearly perfect as could be.

The leaves should be thrown into *boiling* water, with plenty of salt in it—this keeps them a bright green colour. Boil fast for ten or fifteen minutes, then drain and press till firm and dry. In this state most English people consider spinach is quite done ; French cooks think differently. It is now ready to be manipulated in any form desired.

For instance, *Spinach en Croustades* is a pretty way of serving it as a vegetable dish alone, or even as an entrée. The *croustade* is a thick slice of stale white bread, hollowed in the centre, and shaped like a dish with a rim. This is fried to a golden brown in clear fat (if a joint of meat were roasting it might be done in the dripping-tin).

Melt an ounce of butter in a small stewpan,

put in the cooked spinach, add a little pepper, heat well through, beat lightly with a fork, then fill the croustades, and chop a little cooked beetroot to garnish the top.

A purée of spinach with a garnish of poached eggs, or an egg boiled hard, then cut into strips, and a few strips of beetroot interspersed to give colour, is a great improvement to the vegetable plainly boiled. Some thin slices of ham frizzled and placed as a border round a purée of spinach, also makes a very nice dish.

Excellent also is *Spinach à la Crème.* After melting a small lump of butter in the stewpan, and putting in the spinach to simmer, stir in the beaten yolk of an egg, twopennyworth of cream, and a pinch of cayenne pepper. Let it nearly boil, then pour into a rather deep dish, and place fingers of toasted bread round the edge. This is one of the daintiest dishes known.

It has been mentioned before that French cooks often make a " fond " or foundation to a dish of meat with a purée of spinach or sorrel; but it must be remembered that no cream or eggs should be used then, and less butter, substituting the gravy from the meat instead.

Among the lesser known vegetables we may also place *watercress*.

It may sound paradoxical to say that no people consume watercress more largely than do Londoners, and yet to call it a little known vegetable ; yet apart from eating it in its natural state, its capabilities are almost unknown.

Watercress Soup is undreamt of by many people, but it is simple and nourishing, and meets with the approbation of all who try it. As a salad, too, it is much appreciated, either alone or with lettuce, and as a sauce to accompany roast mutton it is frequently used in French houses. Chopped small and laid between thin slices of bread and butter for sandwiches, it is getting to be much favoured at the afternoon tea-table.

Be it remembered, however, that although watercress is most valuable as a medicine, being a gentle stimulant, and strengthening to the nerves, yet from the nature of its growth it requires most careful cleansing, or we may imbibe more harmful properties than we gain good from eating it.

The expressed juice of fresh watercress taken by a teaspoonful at a time, has been found invaluable in cases of throat disease. The German physician, Haller, said that he had seen patients in deep decline cured by living almost entirely on this plant.

The best specimens are those with the bronzed leaves. During the winter and early spring is perhaps the best season for water-cress, but they are good and acceptable all the year round.

Full directions for making the watercress soup will be found at the end of this chapter.

Watercress sauce is made by stewing chopped watercress in butter for ten minutes, then adding a pinch of salt, the same of pepper, the same also of mustard, and a spoonful of vinegar. Beat till quite smooth with a wooden spoon, then add the gravy from the roasting joint. This is served in a sauce-tureen, and is a pleasant change from ordinary gravy.

Almost all the dishes mentioned might come under the category of kitchen-physic,—for one of the first essentials in sickroom diet is to please the eye as well as the palate.

Sorrel Soup (*Potage à l'Oseille*).

Having carefully washed two large handfuls of sorrel, dry it, then chop it finely. Chop also a medium-sized spring onion. Melt an ounce of butter, stew the onion and sorrel in this (in a covered stewpan) for about half an hour. Meanwhile, bring a quart of water to boiling point in the soup-pot, throw into it a slice of stale white bread cut into dice (no crust), and let it boil till the sorrel is ready. Add that next, then a teaspoonful of salt, half one of pepper, and the beaten yolks of two eggs. Let all boil up once, then pour into the tureen. A pinch of dried herbs or just one grate of nutmeg may be added then.

Watercress Soup.

The foundation of this soup is best made from a puré of haricot beans. They should have been soaked overnight, then boiled for two or three hours, or until they will rub through a sieve. Chop the watercress, and cook it in butter with an onion also chopped, as the sorrel was done. Add enough boiling water to the haricot purée to bring it down to the consistency of cream; then stir in the watercress, etc., and any other *green* herb you may possess. Just before serving stir in a tablespoonful of cream, and salt and pepper to season it well. A pint of haricots should be sufficient for a quart of good soup.

CHAPTER XII.

Leeks and Onions.

ALTHOUGH some attention has been paid to the uses of leeks and onions in the previous chapters, yet for their great medicinal and useful properties they merit more particular study.

The wonderful faculty which onions possess of *absorbing* disease germs ought to be written in letters of gold before the eyes of every householder. Merely hanging in a net they will purify an apartment, and a string of onions suspended from the ceiling preserved the inmates of a whole cottage from being attacked by cholera, when the scourge was devastating the whole of the neighbourhood.

Especially in cases of that fell disease diphtheria have they great power. A dish of raw onions *sliced* and set in the sick-room, will draw away the disease and give ease to the sufferer;

as their odour gives out they should be replaced by fresh ones. Poison of any kind will discolour an onion. If one be placed in a dish of mushrooms about whose orthodoxy there is felt the slightest doubt, the suspicion may be quickly removed or proved thereby, as the onion will turn black if they are unwholesome.

They are a stimulant also, rousing and aiding digestion.

Many persons who complain of onions being difficult of digestion would find the objection removed — or considerably lessened — if they were cooked thus : cooking them quickly at the first start, then drawing aside and covering well, allow them to simmer gently for some time ; this draws out the juice, which can be poured off. If treated thus, they will hardly disagree with the most fastidious.

To confess to a liking for onions is—sad to say—considered vulgar, but our French friends are notable as proclaiming their weakness for both onions and garlic by the scent they carry about with them.

Although certainly related to onions *leeks* are not the same, nor even similar. They are more prized in Wales and Scotland than in England, and are very highly esteemed in France, where they are used as a vegetable alone, and never upon any account are they omitted from the potagère.

They have a direct action upon the liver, and in cases of liver complaints (very often also for rheumatism) they are ordered by the doctor, either in the form of a tea or *tisane,* or as a poultice.

The "tea" made by boiling leeks in water may be made very much more palatable for an invalid if a teaspoonful of Bovril or Liebig's Extract be dissolved in each cupful. A liberal seasoning of salt and pepper also helps both taste and tonic.

For broth from beef or mutton it is better to tie the leeks together in bunches, and serve them thus among the other vegetables round the dish,—or, better still, if there be any quantity of them, to serve them separately in a vegetable dish, pouring white sauce over them ; they are both wholesome and delicious if treated thus.

During the winter months they should be kept covered with fresh earth.

A poultice of fresh-boiled leeks laid between flannel is a remedy which certainly comes under the category of kitchen physic. It is a remedy,

however, much trusted by continental doctors
for any inflammation of the liver or kidneys,
and has the power of quickly bringing out
copious perspiration.

The mild flavour of leeks makes them much
preferred in nearly all soups — they combine
with other flavours, but will not overpower, as
the onion too frequently does.

Both leeks and onions make excellent soups ;
if a little clear broth is at hand to use instead
of water, of course the soup will be richer for
it ; bread forms the thickening quality—a slice
of white bread cut into dice and thrown into the
boiling liquor a few minutes before serving it.

There is a very simple soup known as " drunk-
ard's broth," made by boiling sliced onions in
water, which is said to be very valuable and
grateful to persons recovering from intoxica-
tion.

A pinch of mixed sweet herbs is a great
addition to leek or onion soup.

A large white onion, with the core removed
and its place filled with a savoury stuffing, then
placed in a covered stewpan with a little dripping, cooked in the oven for an hour, and a little
thick brown gravy poured over it on the dish,

makes a very savoury and economical little "plat" for a cold winter's evening. The stuffing may be made from any cold meat, minced, and mixed with sharp sauce.

Large white onions, boiled till tender, then drained, sliced thinly into a shallow tin, a few nobs of butter placed over them, a liberal powdering of pepper and salt, then some stale cheese shaved as thinly as possible, and a few bread-crumbs sprinkled over all, placed in a quick oven for ten minutes, makes another cheap savoury.

A small onion may be introduced with advantage into many preparations of meat, fish, poultry, etc., where its presence is not needful nor perhaps desired, because it will help to bring out the flavour of the other condiments, and if sufficiently small, itself pass unnoticed.

For sauces and fine dishes French cooks much prefer to use shallots, their flavour is more delicate. A clove of garlic, too, although a liking for its searching aroma certainly has to be acquired, is yet most suited for use in many made-up dishes.

If the salad-bowl be rubbed all over inside with garlic, before breaking the lettuce or cress

into it, it not only obviates the necessity of
using any onion in the dressing, but gives a
piquant, *elusive* flavouring as difficult to "fix"
as delicious to taste.

Chives, too, belong to the onion family. They
are worthy of much more popular use and cultivation than they can boast at present : the root
is bulbous, and grows up early in the spring,
ready prepared for the "omelettes au fines
herbes," the soupe or salade "printanier"; and
for an addition to forcemeat or stuffing they are
unrivalled.

Thus we see that useful and valuable as onions
are they cannot well do everything, as in this
country they are unfortunately generally expected to.

In many greengrocers' shops,—large ones too
—and on the costers' stalls in the street, leeks
are a rarity, and always expensive; shallots
still rarer, garlic and chives unknown. Even in
the country they are seen in but few gardens;
and it is no uncommon thing to be asked what
is their use. This is a state of affairs which
needs remedying; we are conservative to our
own loss, and, as a nation, remarkably slow to
learn, or add to our knowledge.

P.C.   L

CHAPTER XIII.

Tomatoes.

FROM being one of the least known and most expensive vegetables, tomatoes have become very common and plentiful, bought and eaten on the streets as freely as cherries or apples, and used in the kitchen almost as much as we can desire.

Perhaps never better or more beneficial than when eaten raw, still, to be really nice thus, they ought to be freshly-gathered from the plant; and few persons are able to do this.

Next to eating them raw we may rank eating them "marinées," or "en salade," viz., slicing them in a dish, and dressing with salt and pepper, vinegar and oil. In Parisian restaurants they are served thus all the summer through, and very refreshing and acceptable they are. A small onion sliced with them is an agreeable addition. They are even better than cucumbers if dressed in this manner and served with cold meats.

A purée of tomatoes may be made exactly in the same way as the purée of sorrel or spinach, and served with hot meat. With veal, poultry, sweetbreads, mutton cutlets, or pigeons halved and done on the grill, a purée of tomatoes, highly seasoned and made fairly thick, is a great addition to the dish.

The same purée is invaluable as an aid in using up the remains of cold meat. The latter may be merely sliced and laid in the purée to become hot through, or the slices may be lightly frizzled first.

In winter the tinned tomatoes will answer the purpose excellently well, therefore it is well to have them in reserve : an un-appetising dish of cold meat may be quickly transformed into a delicious savoury by their aid at very short notice. An edging of well-boiled rice is a pretty finish to the dish.

Plenty of seasoning—especially pepper—should be used with tomatoes, a pinch of cayenne is an advantage.

Tomato Soup

is one of the most delicious and most easily
prepared. For this, slice the tomatoes into a
little melted butter in a deep stewpan; let them
cook gently at least half an hour, and meanwhile
cut up a carrot into rounds an eighth of an
inch in thickness, also slice an onion thinly, and
frizzle these till tender through in a separate
vessel. Next strain the tomatoes through a
sieve to keep out skins and seeds, return the
pulp to the stewpan, add boiling water to make
sufficient quantity ; mix a dessert-spoonful of
potato flour with a little cold water, and stir
this in, then add salt, pepper, and pinch of cayenne, according to taste ; let the soup boil up
once, then stir in the carrots and onion. It
may simmer gently for a time, or be served at
once, as is required. A few fried croutons of
bread should be put at the bottom of the tureen.
This soup should be very hot and piquant.

With the same purée of tomatoes before mentioned as a foundation, we may, with little
trouble, make a truly vegetarian dish, and one
which is very pretty to look at. After making
the purée smooth, thick, and savoury, pour it

into a fancy dish, and keep hot while the "snow-balls" are made. Boil a pint of milk with a pinch of salt; beat to a stiff froth the whites of two eggs also with a pinch of salt, then drop this snow by small spoonfuls into the boiling milk; they will swell out, and take but a few moments to cook. Lift them carefully out, let all the milk drain from them, then set on the red purée, and put a sprig of green parsley in the centre of each.

This is called "Snowballs in Tomatoes," and is a very effective dish.

Stuffed Tomatoes

are great favourites with many people. The tomatoes used in this way should be of a fair size. Remove the core and a small portion of the inside, then fill up with forcemeat, sausage-meat, or any nice mince well seasoned. Place them in a well buttered baking-tin, sprinkle a few bread raspings over the top of each, then bake for ten or fifteen minutes, but do not allow the tomatoes to fall.

Tomatoes are very good if simply baked with a little butter, and salt and pepper, but if done *au gratin* they are better still.

After buttering the bottom of the dish, sprinkle upon it a few bread-crumbs, finely chopped parsley, and chives or shallot, then the tomatoes —the core removed—and cover with the same ingredients, having a few more bits of butter for the top of all. Bake for twenty minutes.

Again, with a dish of cauliflower and macaroni, if dressed in the usual manner, and a purée of tomatoes used in place of white sauce, the change would be found very acceptable.

A sliced tomato is a great improvement to any salad, and the smaller ones should always be set on one side for decorative purposes. In a cool place they will keep for some time.

For a *cold* dish, and a very refreshing one, a *Tomato Mayonnaise* is excellent.

If possible, skin the tomatoes, cut them in half, set them in a glass dish, and put on the ice or in a very cold place for half an hour. Make the mayonnaise with the yolks of two hard-boiled eggs and a tablespoonful of vinegar, beaten together to a cream, a pinch of salt and a teaspoonful of made mustard with a pinch of cayenne. Add by degrees a tablespoonful of olive oil. Spread a little of this

mayonnaise over each half tomato, let it cool
still longer, and before bringing to table place
tiny pieces of ice amongst them in the dish.

A Conserve of Tomatoes

to keep in small jars or pots is very useful for
making savoury sandwiches for afternoon tea-
parties. To three pounds of tomatoes allow one
pound of loaf sugar, an ounce of ground ginger,
a pinch of cayenne, a teaspoonful of salt, the
peel and juice of two lemons. Boil the tomatoes
first for twenty minutes, then rub them through
a sieve ; boil next the pulp with the other ingredients for twenty minutes after they have
come to boiling point. Take out the peel of the
lemon, pour the mixture into jars, and cover
tightly when quite cold. Keep in a cool, dry
place.

It is difficult to bottle or *can* tomatoes at home.
For those who are able to procure the right
sort of bottles—with good screw-tops—and who
have a large quantity of tomatoes to use, it
should be remembered that the secret of keeping well depends upon the care of the cook
in having the bottles heated until they can
scarcely be touched, the tomatoes *boiling hot*

when they are put in, and screwing down the tops *at once*, before any heat can have evaporated. The tomatoes should be brought to boiling-point in salted water, and drained before they have time to break.

Tomatoes form an excellent addition to an omelette. They should be cut into quarters, and slightly sprinkled with pepper, then frizzled in the butter before the eggs are added.

The applications and uses of this valuable vegetable-fruit, and the combinations which a clever cook may produce by its aid, are very numerous, indeed well-nigh endless.

CHAPTER XIV.

Mushrooms.

IN town mushrooms rank as do tomatoes amongst the additional luxuries of the table; but in the country, where in their season they are to be had for the gathering, they form one of the poor man's few delicacies. Most people recognise only two distinct classes of them, viz., mushrooms and toadstools, and, through ignorance, many excellent varieties are passed by as unfit for food. The late Dr. Lankester, an eminent authority on foods of all kinds, enumerates no less than *forty* different species of mushrooms, all of which are good to eat.

Chanterelles are much esteemed in France, while the delicate morel is there much more frequently met with than in England; although if sought for at the beginning of summer it

may sometimes be found in our orchards and
woods.

Another good authority on foods says : " Have
nothing at all to do with them, until you are an
excellent judge between the true and the false."
This advice resembles that of the mother who
cautioned her son not to venture near the water
until he had learned how to swim !

Although we can scarcely be too cautious in
our use of all fungi, still, as they are an excellent and delicious article of diet, when good, we
need not be martyrs to our fears.

A peeled white onion thrown into the pot
while they are cooking will speedily confirm or
dispel any fears which may be entertained about
them, so also will a silver spoon, for if poison
lurks within the vessel it will quickly turn the
silver black.

It is chiefly the people who live in the country,
and have the good fortune to gather for themselves, who have much need to exercise caution ;
in town we are mostly supplied with mushrooms
grown from spawn in mushroom houses or frames,
and have little to fear. On the other hand,
country people have full benefit of the flavour

and succulence of a freshly-gathered mushroom which it is difficult to surpass. The best mushrooms are most plentiful in August and September; they grow in open sunny fields after low-lying fogs or heavy dews. The upper surface is a dirty white, *par complaisance* pearl colour, and the under surface salmon or light-brown in colour. They should emit a faint wholesome smell. The Scripture says of the slothful man that " he roasteth not what he took in hunting." The same reproach may be applied to those who neglect or despise the good gifts which Providence places within their reach. A plentiful crop of mushrooms brings many additional pounds into the pockets of the inhabitants of some localities.

For the benefit of those who have the good fortune to possess or meet with a plentiful supply a hint as to their preservation for winter use may prove acceptable.

They must be taken, while perfectly fresh, and skinned, removing the stalk also,—then laid on thick white paper, not touching each other, and dried in a *very* slow oven. They should take several hours, and when quite dry should be threaded on a fine string and hung up in a dry place. They will shrink considerably, but only require to be placed in cold gravy or liquor, then warmed up, to swell out to their original size.

Mushrooms à la Provençale is a way of treating them which is very popular in the South of France.

In a small, shallow frying- or sauté-pan place sufficient salad-oil to cover the bottom to the depth of a quarter of an inch. Let the oil come to boiling point, then slice into it a small white onion, add a tablespoonful of finely minced and *dry* parsley. Next put in the mushrooms—small flat ones are preferable—the skin and stalk removed; sauté them for five minutes, then pour off about half the oil, dust flour over the mushrooms, sprinkle with salt and pepper, add a dash of vinegar, toss them well about for a minute longer, then serve over fried croutons, or crisp thin toast.

For mushrooms à la *Poulette*, pick out the small *white* or button ones. After removing peel and stalk, drop them into boiling salt and water, and cook till just tender through. Drain on a cloth, then place in a shallow dish and cover with the following sauce : an ounce of butter melted, and the same quantity of fine dry flour mixed smoothly with it, or half the quantity of potato flour, a pinch of salt, and a tumblerful of boiling water; boil this well, then draw aside and stir in the yolk of an egg and two spoonfuls of cream. Pour this sauce over the mushrooms, and garnish the dish with parsley.

Mushrooms *au Gratin* are one of the most favoured entreés at grand banquets, — so favoured indeed that it is generally found necessary to provide twice the quantity of this dish in proportion to that of any other entrée.

They are prepared exactly in the following method. A gratin dish is covered at the bottom with an ounce of butter broken into bits, finely minced chives, chervil and parsley are sprinkled on to this, then a few bread-crumbs; next the peeled mushrooms, stalks uppermost, the bread-crumbs and herbs sprinkled over, with half a teaspoonful of pepper, and a glassful of white wine poured over them, and more melted butter last of all. Baked in the oven for twenty minutes, then brought to table in the same dish.

Large flap mushrooms are very delicious if steeped in a "marinade" of salad oil, minced herbs and onion, then drained, sprinkled with pepper and salt, and grilled quickly over a clear fire, first on one side, then on the other, for three or four minutes. One of these, served on a piece of crisp toast, might tempt the appetite of the most fastidious. The deep cup-shaped ones filled with a force-meat stuffing, then baked in a dripping-tin and served in pretty paper cases, make another nice entrée.

Mushroom Omelette

is a delicacy which needs but to be tried to establish its reputation for ever. Whatever size or shape they be, the mushrooms must be peeled and cut into strips, then frizzled till tender in a little butter, dust them with flour to slightly thicken the juice, and sprinkle liberally with salt and pepper. Make the omelette in its own pan, according to the directions previously given; *slide* it on to a hot dish, cover half of it with the mushrooms, then fold over the other half, thus securing the brown side for the upper surface.

For *Mushroom Ketchup*, than which there is no more useful ketchup for kitchen use, the follow-

ing is an excellent recipe. All broken mushrooms, parings and stalks (if clean), should be
placed in a shallow earthen vessel and well
covered with salt. Let them stand for three
days, stirring occasionally. Then draw off the
juice, and to every pint allow half a teaspoonful
of ginger, the same of powdered mace, allspice,
and cayenne. Put in a stone jar, set in a pan
of water, boil hard for six hours, pour into
bottles when cool.

CHAPTER XV.

Fruit "en Salade" and "Glacé."

A FRUIT Salad is most certainly an almost unknown delicacy on English tables. It is most frequently met with in Parisian and Viennese restaurants, where the most critical gourmets do congregate.

Perhaps at its best when made with the wild wood-strawberries, plentiful enough in the woods about Paris, it is also exceedingly good made with the smaller kinds of cultivated strawberries, with raspberries, or raspberries and fine ripe currants, with sliced apricots and peaches, pineapples, and oranges.

Next to a salad of wild strawberries, one of oranges, with a sprinkling of ground almonds, walnuts and grated cocoanut, must take the place of honour.

The *sine qua non* of a successful salad is that

its components should be *dry* before the dressing is added to them, whether the salad be
composed of a vegetable or fruit.

Next to dryness, we must insist upon perfect
ripeness when fruit is in question. Hard or unripe morsels will spoil any dish.

A crystal salad-bowl, or failing that, a deep
compôte dish, is best for the purpose.

Pure white castor sugar, and wine suited to
the kind of fruit used, forms the "dressing."
This should be poured over the fruit at least an
hour before it is brought to table.

In the case of wild strawberries, plenty of
sugar and a little good *Claret* is used, but for
garden strawberries *Port* is preferable to Claret.

With apricots, pineapple, or peaches, use a
light sweet wine, like Sherry or Madeira; and
for an orange salad a raisin wine (Muscatel) is
best suited.

For a pound of fruit allow four ounces of
sugar, and half a pint of wine. Turn the fruit
over occasionally after the dressing has been
added, that it may absorb it thoroughly.

Oranges should have all the peel removed,
especially all the white part, divide them in
their natural divisions and press the pips out.

Skin the walnuts and pound them, the almonds likewise, grate the cocoanut.

A tablespoonful of *liqueur*, say *Prunelle* or *Kummel*, will be an improvement to any fruit salad.

Very ripe blackberries, with a little less sugar, and Port wine or Roussillon, or instead a small tumblerful of Blackberry Cordial and a table-spoonful of Brandy, makes a very wholesome dessert dish.

Fruit may be kept fresh for a length of time by putting it into stone jars and covering with a mixture of honey and water. When required for use, take them out, wash in clean water, and they will be almost as good as freshly-gathered.

A very easy way of candying fresh fruit such as ripe currants in bunches, grapes, etc., is done by taking them by the stalk, dipping into a tumbler containing water and the white of an egg, then rolling them in fine castor sugar and laying on sheets of note paper to dry, either in the sun or in a cool oven.

To candy fruit properly, however, is a much more serious process.

A syrup of boiling sugar, boiled to the fourth
or "candied" degree, that is for at least half
an hour, is the first essential.

Place the sugar,—finest loaf—in an enamelled
saucepan; to half a pound of sugar allow half
a tumblerful of water. Boil until the syrup
is so stiff it will crack if drawn out into
threads.

Supposing you are candying some quarters
of oranges; after taking out the pips, thread
them on a fine string, and passing the string
over a hook hold them in the boiling syrup for
half a minute. Then suspend them to drain
and dry.

Greengages, apricots, cherries, etc., require
to remain in the syrup a little longer, that they
may be cooked through, then they may be
rolled in powdered sugar, and dried in a cool
oven.

Fine scarlet rhubarb cut in strips of two or
three inches in length, dropped into this syrup
for a few moments, then drained and "frosted,"
makes a pretty sweetmeat.

It is by no means impossible for the amateur
cook to turn out a very pretty dish of glazed
fruits for an extra occasion, if needs be,
although as glacé fruit can be bought so reason-

ably now, few amateurs care to attempt the process.

"*Marrons glacés*," the favourite sweetmeat of the few who are able to indulge their liking, are made in this wise (*n.b.* the same process is employed for "*Chinois glacés*," or Chinese green-gages, and for crystallized figs) : The chestnuts are boiled in water until they are quite cooked, then carefully peeled and thrown into cold water to become hard again. In half an hour's time they are placed in boiling syrup, the which has been boiled till quite stiff. The vessel containing them is then set on one side. The next day the syrup (and chestnuts) is brought to boiling point, then put aside to cool again. This process is repeated four days in succession; at the end of the time the chestnuts or fruit will be found to have absorbed nearly all the syrup, and must then be lifted out on to dishes, and dried off.

The process of preserving fruit by evaporation is best performed by means of the mechanical "evaporators" when possible to obtain these machines; still, by carefully drying in a cool oven (a brick oven is best for the purpose), much valuable fruit might be saved for winter use which is often left to rot on the trees because it will not pay for gathering and turning into preserve.

Only *sound* fruit should be dried, and it should be gathered on a dry day, laid out separately on sheets of paper or tins, and dried in the oven when the fire has become low. It will require soaking in water before using.

A word of caution as to the kind of sugar which should be used with fruit, will not be out of place here.

Beet sugars, because of the impossibility of ensuring their perfect dryness, however highly refined, should be avoided; also because they absorb moisture easily and so cause fermentation. For all syrups, jams, jellies, etc., use only pure cane sugar; although slightly more expensive it well repays in the end.

Boiling sugar quickly passes from one degree to another, and in preserving it is important to remember this fact and not add the sugar until the fruit has been first well cooked.

It is the fruit that requires cooking, and not the sugar.

It is a great improvement to jellies to first

heat the sugar in shallow vessels in the oven, before putting into the juice; it should be so hot the hand can scarcely touch it. Put into the juice when that has boiled for twenty minutes, boil up once more after the sugar is dissolved, then pour into *hot* jars at once. It will quickly jelly, and be a better colour than if made after the old method, besides retaining better the flavour of the fruit.

CHAPTER XVI.

Entrées and Entremets.

A VERY large variety of dishes may be classed under the above title, and it is in the preparation of these dishes almost more than in those of any other class that the really experienced cook will best exercise the true principle of cookery-economy.

As a rule the entrée is served before the joint; the entremet follows it.

No Parisian " little dinner " would be considered complete without one entrée at least; and although it may seem a strong statement to make, it is certainly true, that the materials out of which many of the most tempting of these entrées are made are those which in English hotels and even in private houses would be thrown to the dogs, or into the fowl-pen.

It is important to strive as far as possible to

167

make entrées the means of utilising any remains
which may be left. A nice variety can be made
in this way only.

Another important point to observe is the
appearance of the entrée. This class of dishes
may be regarded as one of the higher branches
of the profession, and had better not be at-
tempted by the apprentice. One very common
mistake made by inexperienced cooks in serving entrées is putting too much on one dish.
"Little and good" is an excellent maxim to
follow.

It is very desirable to have certain things
at hand in readiness when making entrées, or
indeed any other class of savoury dishes ; viz.,
aromatic spices, dried herbs, and a little stock
of sauces and seasonings.

Once these are set up in the kitchen it is easy
to keep them renewed, and they prove invaluable
on many occasions, well repaying what little
trouble their preparation entails.

An excellent aromatic preparation is made as
follows :—take equal quantities, say half an
ounce, of mace, nutmeg, cloves, marjoram,
thyme, basil, and bay leaves, a whole ounce of
peppercorns. Have all these thoroughly dried,
and pounded, and sifted, and put in a glass-

stoppered bottle for use. This will keep good for years. The preparation of herbs has been described in a previous chapter.

It is not so much a question of expense in the preparation of entrées as of management.

A good cook will never be embarrassed by having too much cold meat on hand while she has entrées to provide for. By a little skill she will be able to turn out the most charming dishes ; even a small piece of the loin of mutton may be served half a dozen different ways.

One of the most commonly known of entrée dishes is perhaps " croquettes " or " krome-skies," and yet how rarely are they nicely made and served.

The secret, or rather the principle, to be observed in making these is the same as in boiling or roasting meat ; viz., to form a crust on the outside to retain the moisture and juices within. It is generally admitted that these are far nicer when the inside is moist and juicy, instead of hard. A good way to ensure their being so is to moisten the mince with gravy made from bones, which will jelly when it is cold.

The mince may then be made quite thin, and allowed to get quite cold before being shaped into little balls or cutlets, and then twice coated with egg and bread-crumbs, and dropped into boiling fat. The croquettes are thus surrounded with a crust, and if carefully lifted out the moment they are sufficiently cooked, the inside gravy will be preserved.

It may almost be taken as a criterion of the skill of the cook when as soon as the fork of the eater is inserted into the ball the inside gushes out, as it certainly requires some practice to attain to this.

Almost any kind of cold meat may be made into entrées, but cold remains of poultry, or calf's head, or game may be made to look very appetising if cut small, nicely shaped, and then each piece slightly floured and dipped into good batter, when they should be fried a beautiful golden colour.

They will look like fritters, and should be lightly piled on a silver dish if possible, and garnished with parsley.

Another way of using up these remains is to make a "salmi." To do this, the pieces of meat should be sliced thinly and all trimmings and bones be stewed to make sauce. The liquor, when they have cooked long enough, should be strained and slightly thickened, then liberally seasoned and a glass of good wine added to it; Madeira is the most suitable, though sherry will do. The pieces of meat have simply to be warmed up in this sauce.

When making a "hash" from cold meat it is always preferable to make the sauce or gravy first, then add the minced meat, and allow it to simmer only for a few minutes before serving. When made of fresh meat the hash will be found to be much richer and more tender if cooked in the oven slowly.

A nice little dish of hash, with two or three delicately poached eggs laid upon it, and some slender strips of toasted bread round the edge, and a little finely chopped parsley sprinkled over all, will be found to make a very pretty and economical entremet.

"Tomates farcis" is another economical entremet. Smooth, round tomatoes not over ripe should be chosen, and a small piece be cut out of the middle, and a little of the inside removed; its place should be filled with a little forcemeat, or sausage meat alone will do very nicely. Place the tomatoes in a tin with small bits of butter, to bake gently until tender through.

Nice kidney potatoes may be treated in the

same way, and will be found very excellent also.

Eggs "à la bonne femme" make another pretty entrée. Take six large eggs, boil them ten minutes, when cool enough carefully remove the shells, and with a sharp knife split them in half; remove the yolk from each half and the tip of the point, so that they may stand firmly. With the yolk mix a little finely minced ham and beetroot or boiled chicken, a little drop of some piquante sauce, and then fill up the hollows, piling the mixture a little higher. Place the eggs on a bed of curly lettuce or parsley.

Omelets and vol-au-vents are served as entrée dishes. The latter, although properly belonging to the confectioner's profession, and generally considered to be quite beyond the skill of the home cook, may yet be fairly well imitated for any extra occasion.

The exterior or crust is made of the very finest puff paste moulded into the required shape, and the interior hollow is preserved while the crust is cooking by filling it with soft bread; the upper crust is laid over the bread, but the edges are kept from sticking to the sides.

When the crust is baked the bread is removed and the proper filling takes its place, then the upper crust is laid over and glazed with white of egg. This filling may be varied according to fancy—a financière ragoût, sweetbreads, oysters, lobsters, shrimps, etc. When fish is used, the top of the vol-au-vent should be ornamented with the same or similar small fish.

Whatever is chosen for the filling should be cooked in a sauce, thick, rich, and suited to its individual character: oysters, shrimps, fillets of sole, etc., in thick white sauce with cream; ragoûts of meat, poultry, etc., in brown sauce. Button mushrooms are a great addition to the last-named.

Sweet vol-au-vents, made of fruit cooked as for a compôte or jam placed in the hollow and a whipped cream over the top, are very delicious.

The following short lists may be useful as a guide to what are really orthodox and reliable *entrées*. A few selected *entremets* are also appended.

Meat Entrées.

Beef croquettes, olives, croustades.

„   persillades, miroton, curried.

„   minced, grilled and fricassée.

Mutton cutlets *à la sauce piquante.*

„   „   *à la sauce soubise.*

„   „   *au jardinière,* grilled, etc.

Sheep's kidneys *sautés,* with mushrooms.

„   tails *à la sauce tomate.*

„   brains *à la sauce poulette.*

„   feet, stuffed, fried, etc.

Lamb's head *à la sauce poulette.*

„   cutlets *aux fines herbes.*

Veal cutlet *aux petits pois.*

„   „   fricassée.

„   breast *en blanquette,* with capers.

„   sweetbreads, fricassée, *à la sauce tomate.*

Calf's liver, baked en fricandeau, fricassée.

Calf's head *à la poulette,* etc.

Pork cutlets *à la sauce poivrade,* grilled.

„   „   *à la sauce soubise, tomate,* etc.

„   sausages, *aux choux,* à la pureé, etc.

Poultry, roast, fricassée, *au blanc.*

„   in aspic, in mayonnaise.

„   *à la jardinière,* curried, etc.

„   with turnips, *aux petits pois,* etc.

Pigeons *aux choux, aux champignons.*
Ragoût financière.
Rabbit *au blanc, au jambon.*
  ,,   stewed, roast, *à la Tartare.*
Salmis of game :—snipe, partridges, pheasant,
woodcock, quails, etc.
Game pie, hunter's pie.
Chartreuse of game.

Fish Entrées.

Salmon cutlets, mayonnaise, pickled.
  ,,   ,,   with divers sauces.
  ,,   trout, boiled or baked.
Soles *au gratin, aux fines herbes.*
Filleted soles *en aspic, au blanc,* fried, etc.
Sole Normande.
Cod, baked, au gratin, *à la sauce blanche.*
Salt cod *en brandade.*
Mackerel *à la maître d'hotel,* grilled, etc.
Herrings, grilled, pickled, etc.
Whiting, fried, baked, *au gratin au blanc.*
Plaice, filleted, stuffed, etc.

Vol-au-vent, with various fillings.
Petits pâtés chauds.
Timbales.

Rissoles.   Raised pies.

Eggs au gratin, *à la sauce, aux epinards* (with spinach, sorrel, etc.).

Entremets.

Ham, glazed or sliced.

Tongues, glazed or pressed.

Galantines of meat or poultry.

Omelettes, *aux fines herbes, aux tomates.*

   „   *aux champignons, ognons,* etc.

   „   *au sucre, au confiture, rhum,* etc.

Eggs en salade.

Salads of all kinds.

Mayonnaises.

Macaroni, etc.

Haricots *au blanc, à la bonne femme.*

   „   flageolets *au beurre.*

Petits pois.

Cauliflower *au gratin, au fromage,* etc.

Artichokes.   Aubergines.

Chicory, celery, cucumbers.

Asparagus.   Salsify.   Sea kale.

Mushrooms.   Potatoes.

Sweet Entremets.

Œufs à la neige.

Crème renversée, Crème Sambayone.

Charlotte russe.
Soufflées. Crêpes.
Beignets de Pommes, d'abricots, etc.
Meringues. Compotes of all kinds.
Jellies of all kinds.
Fruit salads.

Directions for preparing almost all the dishes here named have been given in different chapters.

With regard to the dishes made from *remains* (a decided feature amongst this class), sufficient have been indicated to enable the average cook to compile and arrange others for herself.

When *tails,* feet, *brains,* etc., are intended to be used, care must be taken to have them thoroughly cleansed and par-boiled, before dressing them in the manner desired.

Kidneys require light cooking when intending to serve them *sautés;* but if stewed or otherwise served they need longer time and gentle heat.

CHAPTER XVII.

The Déjeuner à la Fourchette.

THAT cleverest of Englishmen, Macaulay,
must have had the "Déjeuner à la Four-
chette" in his mind when he said that "An
invitation to breakfast was a proof that one was
held to be good company; people were invited
to dinner very often, but a man must be really
liked when one asked him to breakfast."

This can scarcely be associated with the
modern English breakfast, which, although an
excellent meal in its way, is generally too early,
too hurried, and too business-like to admit of
the sociability which an invited guest would
naturally expect; hence perhaps the more
favourite invitation to lunch, common enough;
sometimes delightful, sometimes not.

It has been argued that people should never
meet socially until dinner-time; tempers are apt

to be too much tried, or nerves too unsteady, until the work of the day is practically over. This may be a very safe rule for acquaintances and friends, allowing exceptions to be made occasionally, but in the family it is different.

In most families there will be found at least one member who will shirk coming down until the very last moment, thereby endangering the certainty as well as the sanctity of the family breakfast; another perhaps is so far beforehand as to have gone from the house before others can fairly begin the meal.

Our French " père de famille " so far recognises this fact that he does not attempt to struggle against the inevitable. Each member is at liberty to follow his own inclinations as early or late as he pleases, provided they will all assemble at " déjeuner," when as a rule hunger will bring all the flock to the family table.

In Parisian families and in the better class provincial households this is the first serious meal of the day. It is partaken of at midday, breakfast consisting of little more than a cup of coffee, frequently served to each member in his own chamber. This midday repast is generally the time for the family chat, when all meet to-

gether for the first time in the day, and have
less restraint upon them than at the more formal
dinner hour.

It is quite a characteristic meal; although
similar to the Englishman's lunch, yet it is not
so much a make-up meal as the latter, when it
is thought lawful to serve up half-finished joints
or tarts in their original form, with little or no
attempt at disguise. No, the Frenchman looks
for his little "plats" to be as daintily presented
as at the more important dinner, and the
"remains," if brought again before him, must
be delicately "réchauffé."

"Potage" is sometimes served at this hour,
and a vegetable purée is mostly chosen, as the
lighter potages and clear soups are preferable
at the late dinner. Dishes of fish, ragoûts,
fricassées, omelettes, etc., are all eminently
suited for the déjeuner.

Both at the déjeuner and the dinner it is
customary in France to have what are termed
"appetisers," either to commence with or to
hand round during the meal, such for instance
as olives, anchovies, oysters, pieces of Dutch
herrings, sardines and radishes.

The last-named are found exceedingly useful
as a break between two rich-flavoured dishes.

Sardines are perhaps the most esteemed commencement for a déjeuner, as oysters are most liked as a preface to a good dinner.

One very effective little appetiser, and admirably adapted to commence a déjeuner with, is made as follows :—Some small round pieces are cut from a stale loaf, then fried a light golden colour in hot fat, and allowed to cool. Some olives are then stewed, and a few anchovies neatly filleted; these last-named are rolled up and slipped into the stoned olives. Next a drop of stiff mayonnaise sauce is placed upon the tiny round of fried bread, the olive is fixed upon this, and another drop of sauce crowns the whole, or a bit of bright aspic jelly.

The mingled flavours of olive, anchovy, and sauce are delicious. Anchovy toast is also a very nice commencement to a déjeuner.

We will now consider a few dishes suitable for a simple family déjeuner, and equally suited for the luncheon table of our English friends. Let us suppose that sardines have been first handed round, as they are available at all times of the year. Nothing but a good piece of bread is required with them. It need not be hinted that this is a very unsubstantial commencement to a meal; remember it is only the appetiser.

We will now seriously begin the meal with "potage à la purée et au croûtons." This is made by first boiling split peas and other vegetables till thoroughly soft, then passing them through the tamis, and adding a sufficient quantity of stock or thin broth to make all of the consistency of cream. Season this well; let it heat again, and while it is doing so, some bread which has been cut into dice is fried in a little butter till brown, then put in the tureen, and the boiling purée poured over just before serving.

If we had chosen, this same potage might have been made of lentils, haricots, or potatoes, all done exactly the same way.

We will presume the ménagère has at hand some cold roast beef, from which she purposes to make "beef olives." She will first prepare a light forcemeat, bread-crumbs, suet, chopped parsley and herbs, an egg to bind the whole, and pepper and salt; a little fine sausage meat is also an improvement.

The roast beef is sliced very thinly, the forcemeat laid in small quantities on each slice, and these are then rolled lightly, fastened with a little skewer, and dipped into egg and bread-crumbs, then fried in hot fat for a few minutes.

After that they are laid in a brown sauce, well flavoured, to cook a few minutes longer. Just before serving a little wine is added to the sauce.

These olives might also have been made of fresh beef, rump steak very thinly sliced, but in that case a little longer time to stew should be allowed.

" Flageolets au beurre " would be excellent either to follow this dish or to serve with it, according to taste.

The flageolets, cooked in water until quite tender, are well drained, then tossed about in the sauté pan with butter, seasoning, and a little chopped parsley added last of all. All the butter in the pan should be served with them. The same remark made in the case of the potage will apply here—viz., haricots, potatoes, etc., are equally adapted to be served in exactly the same way at a déjeuner.

An "omelette soufflée" might now follow. This is made by whisking the whites and yolks of the eggs apart, allowing one for each person, adding powdered sugar in the proportion of a teaspoonful to each egg, and a little lemon juice to the beaten yolks; then beat in the snowy whites.

A shallow baking tin is liberally buttered,

then heated. The mixture is poured in and baked in a quick oven. It will rise very much, and when lightly browned on the top is sufficiently done, and must be served immediately. A little sifted sugar is a sufficient accompaniment.

Cheese, or biscuits and jelly, generally form the closing portion of a déjeuner, sweet dishes being thought rather out of place, excepting as far as they occur in omelettes.

A glass of liqueur is as invariably the final note as a cup of café noir, both here and at the dinner; indeed the "mazagran" or clear black coffee, served in a thick glass tumbler with lump sugar, seems never out of place at any hour of the day.

Although resembling a dinner, in general outline, at least, it will be seen that a déjeuner is a far simpler affair. One dish of meat is considered quite sufficient, with a dish of vegetables or salad to follow it.

If a fish course is preferred, and it consists of a fairly substantial kind, as soles, or mackerel, or cod, then meat may be dispensed with altogether, or the potage may be omitted.

Simplicity should be one of the characteristics of this repast, as elegance and simplicity may safely travel hand in hand.

CHAPTER XVIII.

Menus for Small Dinners.

THERE is one point in connection with the
all-important meal of the day that, in
small households at least, is frequently overlooked—viz., having a menu. It is sometimes
thought to be ostentatious, but this is a great
mistake, and certainly if there be a guest at
the table it is a kindness as well as a duty on
the part of the host to see that one is provided.

Even at the private family table it will often
be found of great service; imagination plays an
important part in the human organization, a
good name going a long way towards bringing
a dish into favour. So many devices are now
obtainable at so trifling a cost that none need
be excused on this account.

A wise housewife will keep the menus which

have once served, making particular note of those which gained the most favour; they will be found of great service in helping her on future occasions.

Too great care can scarcely be given to the appearance of the dinner table. An insufficient supply of bread, or the lack of minor comforts, such as mustard, well-filled salt-cellars, etc., or knives and forks irregularly placed, are quite enough in themselves to spoil the appetite of the moderately fastidious.

Elaborate decorations either of fruit or flowers are only within the reach of the wealthy, but a few fresh flowers, or a little growing plant, may be procured by the most frugal family economist.

Perhaps the prettiest decoration possible is the common field poppy and its attendant grasses, or the autumn bramble leaves, to be had for the gathering. Ivy or holly in winter may be kept fresh for weeks with care.

Due regard should be had to the fact that we eat by the eye as well as by the palate, and by the sense of association as well as by reason. In fact, too great a regard for reason with many people would be thought sufficient to spoil the appetite; they prefer to follow the example of that good old *bon vivant* of anecdote fame who "ate as he pleased."

He had as many things as he liked, and ate of them as much as he could, then with a stiff tumbler of brandy and water he would go to sleep, and " leave them to fight it out amongst themselves."

That sociability at table is an aid to digestion is an undisputed fact, and no one realizes this more than the typical Frenchman.

Having a natural inclination to domesticity, he is much more alive to the amount of trouble involved in the preparation of a good dinner, and is, therefore, prepared to give due and discriminating appreciation to each course ; welcoming with a beaming eye his favourite " sauce " or " civet," as the case may be, until at the last he is left in that delightful state of mind described as " the love of all mankind and toleration of the Chinese."

When giving an order for a dinner a little forethought should be used ; it will save an infinity of trouble.

It is possible to order a dinner, and a small one too, which implies so many saucepans in use that the fireplace could not hold them all ; or many dishes which can only be dressed at the last moment, therefore all claiming the attention of the cook at the same time.

Fried oysters, croquettes, mutton cutlets, and an omelette, would sorely try the most capable cook were they ordered as four entrées together.

Where the ménagère is her own cook, she will be less likely to fall into this error; still, a little thinking beforehand may save even her a good many steps, and considerable anxiety at the crucial time of serving up. Many things, particularly entrée dishes, may be cooked hours before, and then only require to be warmed up.

We will suppose that a family of six to eight persons has to be catered for, and the housewife has to depend largely upon her own two hands for most of the actual work of cooking, and that soup, fish, one entrée, joint, and sweets is to be the menu.

The entrée should generally (if economy has to be studied) be made of the remains of the previous day's joint, if that is sufficiently reduced in size, or something simple, such as omelettes or a vegetable dish.

Whether an entrée is an expense or no largely depends upon the ingenuity of the cook; if the joint is hot and fresh, an entrée preceding it will serve as a damper, and save it from a too

liberal consumption; if it be cold, then the
same entrée will make it all the more palatable.

In sauces, either for fish or meat, one expense
or provision may be made to serve two purposes. For instance, if we have " Sole à la
Normande," and rump steak with oyster sauce ;
half a dozen oysters will serve for both, while
the melted butter may be all made at once, and
divided afterwards ; the same wine also, and the
same seasoning, etc.

If a dish of vegetables is required, and the
soup is a clear stock or bouillon, these vegetables will cook quite as well in the soup, and
increase its flavour; always, of course, excepting such vegetables as cabbage or spinach,
which should boil in clear water by themselves ;
cauliflowers do not give a disagreeable flavour
by any means, but their whiteness could not be
kept if boiled in stock, therefore they also should
be cooked alone.

Where the first part of the dinner claims
much attention and watching, the sweet dishes
should be such as can be prepared in advance ;
then, if the reverse be the case, the meat cold,
and the fish of a simple kind, a little more
elaboration may be given to this course.

As a rule, two fried dishes or two boiled ones

should not appear in the same menu ; of course, there are occasions when it is necessary to make exceptions, but it will be found too great a tax upon one pair of hands.

The following menus may be found suggestive. Recipes are not given here, as they will mostly be found under their respective headings, or at the close of the book :—

No. 1.

Julienne soup.
Sole au gratin.
Roast loin of mutton with turnips and *sauce blanche au persil.*
Omelettes au rhum.
Fruit tartlets.

No. 2.

Bouillon.
Boiled beef, with a " plat de carrottes."
Braised chicken and salad.
Potatoes sautés.
Apple fritters.
Cheese, with croûtons.

No. 3.

Potage au tomates.
Boiled cod, sauce maître d'hotel.
Fricandeau of veal.
Spinach with eggs.
Rice mould and
Compôte of fruit.

No. 4.

Potage au lait.
Croquettes, tomato sauce.
Roast beef.
Peas or haricots au beurre.
Soufflée pudding, with
Chocolate or jelly sauce.

No. 5.

Bisque of crab.
Lobster cutlets.
Braised leg of mutton.
Cauliflower à la sauce blanche.
Lemon meringue pudding.

No. 6.

Vermicelli soup.
Ragout of mutton.
Cold roast beef.
Potatoes à la crème and
Vegetable salad.
Gâteau de riz.

"Hors-d'œuvre," consisting of oysters, olives. radishes, cheese, and butter, may be placed upon the table or handed round. If liked, potatoes may accompany both fish and all meat dishes.

CHAPTER XIX.

Choice Supper Dishes.

WITH families who breakfast at an early hour, and dine in the middle of the day, the need of a fairly substantial meal at supper time is a felt want. And whether the supper dish be a hot or a cold one, it is of first importance that it should be a savoury one, as it is frequently a wearied mind as well as a tired body which asks to be refreshed at this hour.

Many of the dishes described in the previous chapters are eminently suited for supper dishes; particulary those classed under the head of "Fricassées and Réchauffés," and for an appetising way of serving meat cold see the chapter on "Salads."

Kidneys make a very recherché dish for the supper table, either served alone or with a little meat. They are by no means indigestible if

properly cooked.   Kidneys sauté are delicious.
Slice some kidneys about a quarter of an inch
thick, dip each piece into flour. and drop into
a tin containing a little hot fat, cut some nice
bacon into thin strips and frizzle at the same
time.

The kidneys should be turned about in the
hot fat and only given four or five minutes
cooking; pour off all superfluous fat, sprinkle
with pepper and salt, add a tablespoonful of
ketchup or tomato sauce, the same of boiling
water, stir together and pour over a slice of
hot toast.   Serve immediately.

If a veal kidney is to be had, it is very nice
served as "kidney fritters."   It should be previously cooked, then minced finely.   A batter
made with eggs, milk and flour, according to
the amount of the kidney, chopped chives,
parsley and mushrooms (if available), seasoning
and a little spice.   Beat well together, then
melt a small lump of butter in the sauté pan,
pour in the mixture, allow it to set firmly, then
slide it on to a hot dish and set in a very hot
oven for a moment to brown the top.

The fat part of the kidney should be used as
well as the lean, or else a little fat pork with it.

Meat and game pies of all descriptions are

very desirable supper dishes. French pie crust, whether for eating hot or cold, is made as follows :—Into a pound of flour, half a pound of butter is lightly rubbed and a teaspoonful of salt ; this is made into a smooth paste with two eggs beaten and a small quantity of water. The paste should be lightly rolled out two or three times, then baked as soon as possible.

A very fair imitation of game pie may be made with but little expense if care be given to the preparation of the following forcemeat.

Half a pound of calf's liver and the same quantity of fat bacon should be fried till cooked through, then chopped small and pounded finely in a mortar. When thoroughly reduced, add a good teaspoonful of mixed savoury herbs, half one of black pepper, mustard and mace, and a little salt and a few bread-crumbs ; mix smoothly with two yolks of eggs. Line the bottom crust of the pie with slices of fat bacon, then a good layer of forcemeat, and fill up with joints of fowls or ducks, rabbits, or anything most available at the time. It is not at all necessary that it should be game. If all bones which it is possible to remove are taken out, the pie will be so much the better.

Fill up all spaces with forcemeat, lay a little

more bacon at the top, then put on the top crust, brush over with beaten egg and bake. A little strong gravy well seasoned and a little dissolved gelatine added to it should be poured in when it is baked, through a small hole at the top. This pie may be eaten hot, but it is better cold.

Veal with a little sausage meat, or rump steak with mushrooms, or kidneys, and rabbits jointed, are all excellent "fillings" for pies. These pies require careful and thorough baking.

A very savoury hot dish is a Paté of Macaroni. For this half a dozen lengths of macaroni should be broken into small pieces and gently simmered in a pint of boiling water in which an onion and a little salt has boiled. Drain well, in about twenty minutes' time. Place a layer of macaroni at the bottom of a buttered pie-dish, sprinkle grated Parmesan cheese over and a few bits of butter; then cover with pieces of beefsteak which has been previously stewed tender, the gravy thickened and browned and highly seasoned.

Fricasséed chicken, veal cut small, or sweet-breads cut into dice, may take the place of beef, but should all have been previously stewed in good gravy. Another layer of macaroni and a covering of cheese should form a crust at the top ; then bake this paté for about ten minutes in the oven. Serve at once.

Sweetbreads, either fried in eggs and bread-crumbs, fricasséed, or stewed in a brown sauce, are excellent at supper time, and are very suitable for persons of weak digestion. They should always be parboiled in salt and water, then thrown into cold water before being further dressed.

Boiled fish is scarcely a dish for the supper-table, but small fish broiled over the fire with sauce, or "au gratin," or even fried, are all acceptable. Pork meat and sausages should be avoided at this hour by the wise and prudent.

Eggs are thought to be indigestible at night by many people, but if cooked with care they need not be feared.

If done à la Maître d'Hotel they are very savoury. A Spanish onion should be sliced thinly, frizzled slightly in butter, a little flour added, some hot milk, seasoning and chopped parsley; let this thicken. Take some eggs and lightly poach them ; then lay on toast, and pour this sauce over them.

Eggs may be fricasséed by first boiling them hard ; then cutting them into slices and tossing them in the sauté pan with butter, parsley, seasoning, etc., and adding a little cream, or, if preferred, a little gravy. Amongst French people omelettes are much favoured as a supper dish.

Cheese has rather a bad reputation with many people. If they would take the trouble to grate it and "sandwich" it between bread and butter, they would find it as harmless as it is tasty, and the recommendation given in Chap. IX. is worthy of attention.

"Cheese fondue" is a capital way of using up stale crusts of cheese, besides being another hot and savoury dish.—See Chap. IX.

Cheese and cauliflowers, cheese and macaroni, cheese patés and cheese straws, are all much-liked dishes at the supper table.

Where pastry is objected to, its place may be substituted by a light mixture of eggs, flour, butter, with a pinch of baking powder; the former ingredients in the proportion of a spoon-ful of flour and half one of butter to each egg, and a spoonful of milk. This may be baked in small buttered cups, or it may be poured on to two buttered plates and baked, jam or jelly being spread upon one while the other forms a cover, or it may be baked in one tin as a flat sheet, then spread with jam or marmalade, and rolled up as for a Genoese roll.

Sponge biscuits spread with jelly, placed in a glass dish, and a sweet custard or egg cream poured over, makes a very nice cold sweet dish.

CHAPTER XX.

Addendum.

Some strictly French recipes not included in former chapters.

Potage aux Marrons. *(Chestnut soup.)*

AFTER having boiled the chestnuts, peel them carefully and pound them in a mortar. Pass them through a sieve, adding a little bouillon or clear stock from time to time. When reduced to a purée add more stock to make the quantity of soup required; add salt, cayenne pepper, and mace to flavour it pleasantly. Boil it up again, then if a white soup is desired, add a teaspoonful of boiling cream; if a brown soup be preferred, add a little good gravy and a spoonful of brown thickening. Pour over a little fried bread in the tureen.

200

Potage au Potiron. (*Pumpkin soup.*)

Take a quarter of a pumpkin, if very large a thick slice will be sufficient, pare it, take out the seeds. Then boil in water till quite soft, drain all water away and add a lump of butter the size of an egg, a little salt, then mash well together. Add a pint of boiling milk and a few lumps of sugar, stir well, and when cooled a little stir in a beaten yolk of egg. Pour over a slice of white bread, cut into dice and serve.

Potage Printanier. (*Spring soup.*)

Take a pint of fresh shelled peas, a shred lettuce, cress, parsley, a sprig of mint, a few leaves of sorrel, a few fresh onions, and cook them till tender in a little fresh butter. Press through a colander and add clear stock, let it boil again, then allow to cool, after which add the yolks of three eggs well beaten. Season it well before serving.

Potage aux Poireaux. (*Leek soup.*)

This may be made with either stock or water. A dozen leeks should be sliced thinly, then frizzled in butter till of a nice brown colour, when a slice of bread should be added to them.

Pepper and salt liberally. Let this cook slowly for a little time, then add boiling water or stock to make a sufficient quantity. If liked milk may be used instead.

Potage à la Crécy.   (*Superior carrot soup.*)

Slice and chop small the best part of three or four large carrots, put them into a stewpan with two ounces of butter, add a sliced onion, a turnip, some pepper and salt, a slice of lean bacon, also cut very small. Let them cook for half an hour, shaking the pan occasionally to keep from burning. Pour over two pints of stock or water, let them boil for two hours longer. Strain and press the vegetables through a sieve. Thicken with a tablespoonful of tapioca, return to the pan and boil a few minutes longer. Serve with toasted strips of bread.

Boubillasse.   (*A Provençal potage.*)

Take any kind of fish, but whiting or cod and dory are preferable. Put the fish into a stewpan to boil gently. In a frying-pan place a sliced onion, a clove of garlic, chopped parsley, chopped lemon rind, salt and pepper, spice, and a little oil. When sufficiently fried add the fish, which

should be boned, skinned and cut into quarters.
Stir well together, add two pints of boiling
water and a bit of butter mixed with sufficient
flour to thicken the whole. Let it boil gently
for a quarter of an hour, then serve. If mackerel, sardines, or other rich kinds of fish are
used, make them brown by frying, add clear
stock and a little brown thickening.

Bœuf à la Mode.

A piece of the round of beef is best for this
dish, as there is no bone in it. Lard it with long
strips of salted pork inserted in a larding needle.
At the bottom of an earthenware stewpot or the
" braisière " put first a glassful of white wine,
then several small onions left whole, carrots cut
in slices, a few more bits of salt pork, a " bouquet garni," some peppercorns and a little salt.
Place the meat upon these, cover over tightly
and put the vessel to cook over the charcoal
stove or in the far corner of the oven. Let it
stew gently for five or six hours. Serve with
the vegetables. If the beef is intended to be
eaten cold a calf's foot or small piece of knuckle
of veal should be cooked with it. When the
meat has cooked sufficiently, take it out, take
away the vegetables, and add a beaten white of

egg to clarify the gravy; let this boil for a moment, then strain over the beef; it will jelly when cold.

Langue de Bœuf à la Persillade.

Allow a tongue to boil in salted water until tender; then strip it of the skin and cut it open lengthways down the middle; lay it flat upon a dish. Pour over it a sauce made of butter melted, a wineglassful of vinegar, a good tablespoonful of chopped parsley, pepper and salt.

Langue de Bœuf en Hoche Pot.

Partly boil the tongue in salted water, skin it, cut into short thick pieces. Put into a stew-pan with a few pieces of fat bacon all sorts of vegetables cut into convenient lengths, a bouquet of herbs, seasoning and a glass of white wine. Cover well and cook gently for two or three hours; arrange all neatly on a hot dish, strain the gravy, and pour over all.

Bœuf au Four. (*To be eaten cold.*)

Mince finely a slice of lean beef, then add a small quantity of beef fat, also finely minced,

the same of lean ham, some parsley, mushrooms
(fresh or tinned ones), shallots, and savoury
herbs, all finely minced also. Line a mould with
a few slices of nice bacon, cut small. Add to
the mince four yolks of eggs, to bind it well
together, then put into the mould and bake
gently two or three hours. The mould should
be carefully covered over with a paste made of
flour and water. When sufficiently cooked remove this crust and pour a little melted butter
over the top of the meat. Set aside till cold.
This is a nice dish for the supper table.

Queue de Bœuf en Hoche Pot.

The ox tail is jointed, then parboiled and
cooked afterwards in the stewpan in exactly the
same manner as the "Langue de bœuf en hoche
pot."

Queue de Bœuf à la Matelote.

Cut the ox tail at each joint, stew gently in
the oven with water till quite tender. Make a
little brown roux with butter and flour, and mix
a little of the liquor from the stewpan with it.
Place the joints of ox tail in this and a few
small onions previously boiled in water; add a

glass of wine, a bunch of sweet herbs, a clove, peppercorns, and a spoonful of salt. Cook slowly another hour, take out the pieces of tail, put them on a dish, and arrange the onions round them; strain the sauce, and add a spoonful of capers or anchovy sauce. Pour over all and garnish with strips of fried bread.

Carré de Mouton aux Concombres.

Take a square piece of mutton (a flank cut will do), trim it neatly, prick it with fat all over, then roast it. While it is roasting prepare two or three small cucumbers, which have been pared and steeped in vinegar. Cut them into dice, put a little butter into a stewpan, and a slice of ham; add the cucumbers, and stir them about till they begin to brown, then stir in a pinch of flour with seasoning, a little clear stock. Let them cook a little longer till slightly thick; then pour on the dish and place the roast mutton over.

Carré de Mouton à la Ravigote.

A piece of the breast is best for this. Cut it into small portions, sauté them in a little clear fat for a few minutes, add a spoonful of flour and a cupful of stock; add seasoning and garlic, if liked; if not, a few shallots. Let it simmer for an hour. Then remove all fat; take away part of the sauce, to which add two yolks of eggs and a lettuce, a handful of cress, tarragon leaves and parsley, mint and thyme, all of which have been boiled a few minutes in water and then chopped finely. Stir all this over the fire till it thickens, then arrange the meat on a hot dish, and pour the sauce over it.

Filet de Mouton à la Maître d'Hôtel.

The loin of mutton should have the bones removed for this dish. Lay the piece flat, then place upon it a mixture of minced parsley, herbs, shallots, and a few bread-crumbs; then roll up carefully and fasten securely with small skewers. Place in a baking-tin, with a liberal supply of fat. Let it cook briskly for an hour or more, according to size. Then pour off all fat, add a cupful of stock, a dash of vinegar, a spoonful of dried parsley, pepper, and salt, and a little flour to thicken it. Allow this to boil well, then pour over the roll and serve.

Epaule de Mouton à la Turque.

Boil a shoulder of mutton in a little bouillon or broth with a bunch of savoury herbs, a bit of garlic, a clove, a laurel leaf, basil, two onions, thyme, and a few root vegetables, till just done, allowing a quarter of an hour to a pound weight of meat. A little while before serving take a small quantity of this bouillon, remove all fat, and put in it a quarter-pound of well-washed rice to cook till soft. Put the shoulder of mutton on to a dish, make a few incisions in it to receive the rice, cover the whole completely with rice, and over that grate some stale cheese. Hold a salamander over it to brown the surface, and serve with clear brown sauce.

Haricot de Mouton.

Cut up two pounds of breast of mutton or the blade part of the shoulder; fry the pieces in clear hot fat after first dipping each piece in flour, then drain them when of a nice brown colour; after which cut up some turnips into finger lengths, brown them also in the fat. Then make some clear brown sauce and place the pieces of mutton in it to stew with a bouquet garni, two or three whole onions; then add the turnips. When cooked (in about half an hour) remove the fat. Serve on a hot dish and cover over with the turnips and sauce.

Gigot de Mouton Farci.

Bone a leg of mutton and in the place of the bone put the following stuffing : lean ham, a little salt pork, mushrooms, and cucumbers, minced together, seasoned with salt, mixed spices and savoury herbs mixed firmly together with an egg. Fill up all spaces in the leg with this, tie together with string to keep in place, then put into a covered stewpan with a cupful of broth and one of wine, an onion, a carrot, and a parsnip. Let it cook slowly for two or three hours, strain the gravy, remove all fat, thicken very slightly and serve with the mutton. Or if to be eaten cold, make a glaze of the gravy, and pour carefully over the leg when nearly cold.

Blanquette de Veau.

This is made of the remains of roast fillet of veal. Cut the meat into small equal-sized pieces. Take two teacupfuls of velouté or white thickened sauce, add the yolks of two or three eggs, a small lump of butter, and a pinch of chopped parsley, with the juice of a lemon and a little seasoning. Let the meat thoroughly heat through in this sauce, then serve at once.

If made with fresh meat, it should have been cooked through in a little first. Blanquettes of lamb, poultry, etc., are all made the same way. Add tinned mushrooms if available.

Foie de Veau à l'Italienne.

Cut the liver into small slices and place in a covered stewpan in the following order; a layer of liver, each piece having been dipped into flour, then a liberal sprinkling of the following mixture :—salt, pepper, olive oil, minced fine herbs, mushrooms, garlic or shallots. Continue to alternate with layers of the liver and this mixture till all the liver is used. Let it cook slowly for an hour or two. Remove the meat, add a spoonful of vinegar and a little brown thickening to the sauce, a glass of wine, and serve very hot over the liver.

Foie de Veau à la Bourgeoise.

Keep the liver in one piece, but lard it thickly with fat bacon, cover with flour and place in a stewpan with a little fat, herbs, seasoning and a few shallots. Let it cook three hours. A glass of red wine and a yolk of egg are added to the gravy before serving. Or a cupful of stock may be substituted for the latter, and a

little more flour added if not thick enough.
The liver should be served in thin slices. It is
an excellent way of cooking this portion of the
animal.

Jambon à la Broche.

Take a ham which has been salted and dried,
but not smoked, or a leg of fresh pork may be
used instead. Let the ham steep for twenty
hours in white wine in which an onion and a
bunch of parsley are also steeping. Then lift
it out and set to roast before a clear fire, basting
with this liquor. Before it is quite cooked
through remove the rind, then allow it to brown ;
meanwhile in a saucepan prepare a glaze from
stock made from bones and remains of meat,
clarify and thicken this to form a stiff transparent glaze, and pour over the ham. Serve either
hot or cold.

Jambon à la Braise.

Hams cooked in the braisière are very superior to boiled hams. A few vegetables may be
placed in the pot, if liked, and half a bottle of
wine may be added, but this is quite optional.
A leg of fresh pork will be very much improved
if done this way, but a liberal seasoning and

powdering of flour should be given from time to time. Allow several hours to cook, and if not brown enough remove the cover and set the leg to finish before the fire.

Cotelettes de Porc en Ragout.

The pork cutlets having been previously partly cooked in a stewpan, drain them and brown in butter; add to them a sweetbread cut small, some tinned mushrooms and giblets of poultry, if any are available. Add a little flour, salt, pepper, a bunch of parsley and herbs, minced onion, and a cupful of liquor from the stewpan, and let them simmer gently for half an hour. Cutlets are very nice served over a purée of lentils or peas. For this they should be cooked as above, omitting the ingredients of the sauce, as the latter is not required with a purée.

Lapin au Gîte.

After having skinned, cleaned and paunched the rabbit, make a stuffing, using the liver and kidneys, chopping them finely with a few mushrooms, parsley, chives, bread-crumbs and an egg beaten well, and salt and pepper. Fill the body of the rabbit, sew together again, truss the legs and shoulders with the help of wooden skewers. Lay in a stewpan, pour over a glass of red wine, a cupful of stock, dust it with flour, add a few small onions, a slice or two of fat bacon, and let it cook a couple of hours. Thicken and brown the gravy before pouring over the rabbit.

Lapin en Assiette.

Cut up the rabbit into small joints, partly cook them in a covered vessel with a little stock well seasoned, then lift out the pieces, roll them in egg and bread-crumbs, then in a little melted butter, and either grill them or fry carefully with a little fat. Serve them without gravy accompanied by a salad.

Filets de Lapin en Salade.

The remains of a rabbit either roasted or baked are used for this dish. Cut into small thick pieces. Cut up also two or three anchovies, small onions previously boiled, whole capers, a small quantity of bread cut into " fingers " and fried brown. Dress the whole as a salad.

Lapin Sauté à la Minute.

Cut a rabbit into small pieces, wash and wipe dry. Brown each piece in the sauté pan with butter, aromatic herbs (ground), pepper, salt and mace; add finely chopped parsley and shallots. Draw aside from the fire, cover over and allow to simmer for a few minutes, then serve on a hot dish.

Poulets à la Montmorency.

Draw and singe two chickens of equal size. Mix together minced suet, bread-crumbs, spice, aromatic herbs, pepper, salt, and the juice of a lemon; put a little in the body of each chicken. Lay some thin slices of fat pork over each, and also at the bottom of an earthenware stewpot. Place the chickens upon them, add several carrots, onions, a clove or two, bay leaves, thyme, and a bunch of parsley. Moisten with a cupful of bouillon. Lay buttered paper over all and cook in the oven from two to three hours. Serve with clear sauce espagnole.

Poulets à la Jardinière.

Pluck and draw the chicken. Cut it open down the back and lay as flat as possible. Let

it steep awhile in melted butter in which a clove
of garlic and some strong seasoning has lain.
Then drain the chicken, roll it well in bread-
crumbs, then broil over a clear fire. When
cooked lay upon a hot dish and pour over a
sauce made with a little of the melted butter,
slightly thickened with flour, a glass of wine, a
spoonful of vinegar, chopped parsley and mushrooms. Pour over the chicken and serve.

Poule à la Reine.

Draw and singe a fowl; an old one will do.
Rub it over well with butter, and cover with
sliced lemons. Let it cook for two hours in a
covered vessel, in which place also a carrot, two
onions, a bouquet garni, and a spoonful of vinegar with a little stock. Serve without these
vegetables, but with a sauce made from fresh
tomatoes (see Sauces) or a Financière ragoût.
(See Fricassées and Réchauffés.)

Canard aux Navets.

After having drawn and singed a duck, truss
it, and then place it in a thick brown sauce to
boil gently, turning it about occasionally; add
a bouquet garni, coarse salt and peppercorns, and

some turnips cut neatly into short thick pieces. Allow it to cook from an hour and a half to two hours. Skim away all fat, serve with the turnips piled round the duck. This is the *façon bourgeoise* of preparing the duck. Another way is to cook the duck separately in a white sauce, the turnips boiled in water to blanch them, then added to a little veal stock and white thickening, well seasoned, then poured over the duck when that is thick enough.

Canard à la Purée Verte.

Cook a pint of peas with chives, parsley, and watercress in a little water till quite soft. At the same time boil a duck in broth with aromatic herbs, onions, spice, and seasoning. Pass the peas through a tamis, thin the purée with a little broth, season well, and pour over the duck. A little salt bacon cut in strips and frizzled may be laid round the dish as a garni.

Pigeons en Surprise.

Take five pigeons, pluck and draw them, truss them also. Blanch the pigeons for a few minutes in boiling water. Take them out, and in the same water put five good lettuces. Let them boil ten minutes, throw them into cold water and then squeeze them in a cloth. Cut them in two without separating the leaves, sprinkle the inside with the following mixture : the livers finely minced together with parsley, tarragon, thyme, chives, etc., and all mixed with a little butter, salt and pepper. Then put in each lettuce one of the pigeons, cover with another sprinkling of herbs, and close up the lettuce to appear as if untouched, tie them securely and let them stew in rich broth for an hour. When cooked drain them, remove the string. Serve with a rich sauce made from a little of the liquor thickened with yolks of eggs. Dress nicely on a hot dish and pour the sauce round the "lettuces."

Morue à la Provençale.

Allow some salted cod to lie in water for thirty-six hours, changing the water frequently. Then put on the fire in clear cold water, and as soon as it boils the cod is cooked ; lift it at once and drain it. Place in a tin baking dish some minced shallots, chives and parsley, sliced lemon, a little butter, and two spoonfuls of oil. Arrange the cod over this in small pieces ; then cover over the cod with the same mixture and grate a little stale bread over all. Bake for twenty minutes in the oven.

Morue Fraîche aux Fines Herbes.

Take a whole cod, well wash and clean it. Dry and powder it with flour, then rub over a tin baking-dish with fresh butter. Place the cod in it, pour melted butter over and bake for twenty minutes to half an hour. When done pour over the following sauce :—a lump of butter the size of an egg, a glass of white wine, a tablespoonful of vinegar, same of chopped parsley, chives and sweet herbs, pepper and salt. Let these boil a moment, place the cod on a dish and cover with the sauce. Cod is very good baked this way and served with tomato sauce.

Harengs à la Maître d'Hôtel.

Clean well some herrings, split and bone them; broil them over a clear fire, then lay on a hot dish, spread over them butter mixed with dried parsley, salt and pepper. Squeeze the juice of a lemon over just before serving.

Harengs à la Sainte Menehould.

Split and bone the herrings, let them lie in a little milk for two hours, dry them, then dip into a mixture of melted butter, yolks of eggs, salt and pepper and sweet herbs, cover them with brown crumbs of bread, fry gently and serve with white wine vinegar.

Carrottes en Sauce.

Cut some carrots into thin slices lengthways, and boil in salt and water till tender. It is better to boil them whole and slice them after-wards. Melt some butter in a saucepan, add a little flour, lay in the carrots, season well, pour on to a dish, sprinkle with finely chopped or dried parsley. Celery, parsnips, chicory, and turnips may all be done the same way.

Pommes-de-Terre à la Crème.

Boil some potatoes in water till quite tender, slice them, and put in a saucepan with butter, parsley and chives minced, salt and pepper, and a cupful of cream. Let them boil gently, and beat all the time with a wooden fork.

Salsifis Frits.

Boil the salsifys in water with vinegar and salt till quite tender. Drain and dip them in batter as prepared for apple fritters, then cover with bread raspings, drop into boiling fat, and cook for five minutes. Or they may be boiled, drained, then covered with white sauce.

Betteraves Fricassées.

Pare and slice some beetroots, put them in the sauté pan, with butter, chives and parsley, chopped, a little garlic or minced shallots and a sprinkling of flour, pepper and salt and a dash of vinegar. Let them boil up for a few minutes, then serve. Very good with either boiled or baked beef

Champignons à la Crème.

Place some mushrooms in the sauté pan, with the same addition as above, add a little warm water; when cooked add the yolks of two or three eggs, and a cupful of cream. Let it boil once, and then serve over fried bread.

Pudding à la Moelle.

Break four ounces of dried biscuits into a glass of milk, mix with this the yolks of four and whites of two eggs. Add two ounces of powdered sugar, the marrow of a beef bone minced, a glass of brandy, one of liqueur, and a spoonful of potato flour. Let it boil till thick, then pour into a buttered mould and bake half an hour.

Pets de Nonne.

Put in a saucepan two teacupfuls of water, a little sugar and essence of lemon. Gradually sift in some flour, stirring all the time, add a small lump of butter, and when a smooth paste is obtained, take off the fire, and stir in two eggs thoroughly. Take small portions no larger than a walnut, drop into boiling fat, let them attain a golden colour, drain and roll in powdered sugar. Serve with jelly.

Gâteau d'Amandes.

Weigh several eggs in their shells, add the same weight of flour, butter and white sugar. Pound the same weight of sweet almonds in a mortar with a little lemon juice. Beat the eggs, whites and yolks, together, add them to the almonds, then the other ingredients. Mix all smoothly together. Butter a shallow mould and pour in the mixture. Bake in the oven for twenty minutes. This makes an excellent foundation for fancy cakes.

Compôte Blanche de Pommes.

Pare and quarter some russet apples, drop them into boiling water with a few lumps of sugar in it. Let them cook till tender through, but not broken. Arrange in a glass dish, then add more sugar to the liquor to form a syrup, and boil till it thickens, then pour over the apples.

Pears may be blanched and done the same way. Apricots done the same should have a glass of sweet wine added to the syrup, and the kernels should be blanched and thrown into it, then poured over the fruit.

INDEX.

Q

A SELECTION FROM

WARD, LOCK & BOWDEN'S
LIST OF
STANDARD REFERENCE VOLUMES,
AND
POPULAR USEFUL BOOKS

Price

7/6

THE NEW EDITION OF
THE BEST COOKERY BOOK IN THE WORLD.
(Published November, 1888).

Enlarged, Re-composed, Revised, Improved. With New Menus,
New Modes, New Recipes, New Tables, New Engravings,
New Coloured Plates.

538th Thousand, strongly bound, half-roan, price **7s. 6d.**; cloth gilt·
bevelled boards, gilt edges, **8s. 6d.**; half-calf, **10s. 6d.**;
elegant full tree calf, **18s.**

MRS. BEETON'S
BOOK OF
HOUSEHOLD MANAGEMENT.
Entirely New and greatly Enlarged and Improved Edition,
INCLUDING
**360 additional pages of New Recipes and New Engravings, or in all
about 1,700 pages, with Thousands of Recipes and Instructions,
Hundreds of Engravings and New Coloured Cookery Plates.**

With Quantities, Time, Costs, and Seasons, Directions for Carving
and Trussing, Management of Children, Arrangement and Economy of
the Kitchen, Duties of Servants, the Doctor, Legal Memoranda, and
Bills of Fare and Menus of all kinds and for all Seasons.

*In this New Edition the size of the pages has been increased,
and 360 pages added, so that the work now contains nearly
one half as much matter again as the old edition.*

OPINIONS OF THE PRESS ON THE NEW EDITION.
" Perfect as it was before, it is much more so now."--BRISTOL TIMES.
" Should be one of the wedding presents of every bride."—THE
CHRISTIAN WORLD.
" Hardly anything belonging to domestic life is wanting to this ency
clopædic volume."—MANCHESTER EXAMINER.

*** As a Wedding Gift, Birthday Book, or Presentation Volume at
any period of the year, Mrs. Beeton's " Household Management" is entitled to the very first place. The book will last a lifetime, and save
money every day.*

WARD, LOCK & BOWDEN, Limited.

STANDARD COOKERY & HOUSEKEEPING BOOKS.

Price 3/6

MRS. BEETON'S EVERY-DAY COOKERY AND HOUSE-KEEPING BOOK.
Re-written and Revised throughout, greatly Enlarged and Improved; containing 570 **Pages, 1,800 Recipes,** including Instructions for Foreign and Vegetarian Cookery, New French and English Menus for every Month in the Year, New Menus for Breakfast, Luncheon, Tea, Supper and Picnics, New Tables of Housekeeping Accounts and Household Expenditure, **New Coloured Plates and 600 Engravings.** Large crown 8vo, cloth gilt, *3s. 6d.*

MRS. BEETON'S EVERY-DAY COOKERY *has the reputation of being the best Cookery Book issued at its price, and the Publishers trust that in its enlarged and improved form it may be more acceptable than ever in English-speaking households. Infinite pains have been taken in the preparation of this New Edition. Every line has been recomposed, and Three Hundred Pages added, so that the work will, it is hoped, deserve the praise bestowed upon it of being the Best and Cheapest, as well as the most Complete Manual on Cookery and Housekeeping ever offered at anything like the price.*

2/6

MRS. BEETON'S ALL ABOUT COOKERY.
Enlarged, Revised, and thoroughly brought up to date, containing 2,000 Recipes for every branch of Cookery, New Menus for all meals for all months in the year **Valuable Coloured Plates and 500 Illustrations.** Crown 8vo, 450 **Pages,** cloth gilt, *2s. 6d.*

The Improvements and Additions made in the New Edition may be described under the following head. : — The thorough Revision of all the Recipes contained in the last Edition — New Recipes for every branch of Cookery — The newest modes of serving Dinners and other meals shown in the New Menus — Floral and other pretty Designs for Menu Cards — Table Decorations for all Seasons, being practical suggestions for the Beauty of the Home — The new and beautifully executed Coloured Plates, new Full-page and other Illustrations.

A COMPANION VOLUME TO "MRS. BEETON'S BOOK OF HOUSEHOLD MANAGMENT."

7/6

MRS. BEETON'S HOUSEWIFE'S TREASURY OF DOMESTIC INFORMATION.
With **numerous** full-page **Coloured and other Plates, and about 600 Illustrations in the Text.** Crown 8vo, half-roan, *7s. 6d.*; half-calf, *10s. 6d.*

Among the subjects treated of will be found: — How to Build, Buy, Rent, and Furnish a House. — Taste in the House. — Economical Housekeeping. — Management of Children. — Home Needlework, Dressmaking and Millinery. — Fancy and Art Needlework. — The Toilet. — Modern Etiquette. — Employment of Leisure Hours.

" In the one thousand and fifty-six pages in this marvellous ' Home Book' there is *not one worthless or unnecessary item,* not one article we would ever wish to forget." — THE COURT JOURNAL.

7/6

SYLVIA'S FAMILY MANAGEMENT.
A Book of Thrift and Cottage Economy. With **numerous Coloured and other Plates and 350 Illustrations in the Text.** Medium 8vo, cloth gilt, bevelled boards, *7s. 6d.*

The subjects treated of include: Choice of a Home — Furnishing — Cookery and Housekeeping — Domestic Hygiene — Dress and Clothing — Children — Household Pets and Amusements, &c. &c.

From the SATURDAY REVIEW : " *The most important* publication, so far as variety of subjects is concerned, *which we have yet seen for the benefit of families of small means.*"

WARD, LOCK & BOWDEN, Ltd.

STANDARD COOKERY & HOUSEKEEPING BOOKS.

Price	
2/6	**THE COOKERY INSTRUCTOR.** By EDITH A. BARNETT, Examiner to the National Training School for Cookery, &c. Illustrated. The reasons for Recipes, which are almost entirely omitted in all Modern Cookery Books, are here clearly given. Crown 8vo, cloth gilt, *2s. 6d.*; Cheap Edition, cloth limp, *1s.* "THE COOKERY INSTRUCTOR, we are sure, will be a boon to thousands. It is simple, concise, intelligible and accurate."—SHEFFIELD TELEGRAPH.
2/6	**GOOD PLAIN COOKERY.** By MARY HOOPER, Author of "Little Dinners," "Every Day Meals," &c. This work, by an acknowledged Mistress of the Cuisine, is specially devoted to what is generally known as *Plain* Cookery. Crown 8vo, cloth gilt, *2s. 6d.*; Cheap Edition, cloth limp, *1s.*
2/6	**THE ART OF PASTRY-MAKING :** French and English ; including Cakes, Sweetmeats and Fancy Biscuits. By EMILE HERISSE, late Chief Pastrycook-Confectioner. With 40 Illustrations. Crown 8vo, linen boards, bevelled, *2s. 6d.* *The want of a cheap and reliable Book of Recipes for making Pastry has long been seriously felt by Cooks, Pastrycooks and Housewives. The author has endeavoured to present, in a style so plain and minute as to be perfectly comprehensible to anyone, the newest and bes. recipes, and those only of really practical value. Every recipe in the book has been thoroughly tested and frequently used by the author during twenty years' practice in London and Paris.*
1/– 1/6	**MRS. BEETON'S COOKERY BOOK.** NEW AND ENLARGED EDITION, containing upwards of 1,000 Recipes, 350 Engravings, and Four Coloured Plates. Marketing, Vegetarian Cookery, Menus, Table Arrangements, Trussing, Carving, &c., &c. with Quantities, Time, Cost and Seasons. Crown 8vo, cloth, *1s.*; cloth gilt, *1s. 6d.*
1/–	**THE PEOPLE'S HOUSEKEEPER.** A Complete Guide to Comfort, Economy and Health. Comprising Cookery, Household Economy, the Family Health, Furnishing, Housework, Clothes, Marketing, Food, &c. &c. Post 8vo, cloth, *1s.*
6d.	**THE ECONOMICAL COOKERY BOOK,** for Housewives, Cooks, and Maids-of-all-Work; with Advice to Mistress and Servant. By Mrs. WARREN. NEW EDITION, with additional pages and numerous Illustrations. Post 8vo, limp cloth, *6d.*
6d.	**THE SIXPENNY PRACTICAL COOKERY AND ECONO-**MICAL RECIPES. Comprising Marketing, Relishes, Boiled Dishes, Vegetables, Soups, Side Dishes, Salads, Stews, Fish, Joints, Sauces, Cheap Dishes, Invalid Cookery, &c. *6d.*
6d.	**MRS. BEETON'S SIXPENNY COOKERY BOOK** for the people and Housekeeper's Guide to Comfort, Economy and Health. Crown 8vo, linen covers, *6d.*
6d. 3d.	**MRS. BEETON'S COTTAGE COOKERY BOOK.** Containing Simple Lessons in Cookery and Economical Home Management. A Guide to Economy in the Kitchen, and a valuable Handbook for Young Housewives. Fcap. 8vo, cloth limp, *6d.*; paper covers, *3d.*
1d.	**BEETON'S PENNY COOKERY BOOK.** Containing more than 200 Recipes and Instructions. Price *1d.*; post free, *1½d.*

WARD, LOCK & BOWDEN, Ltd.

EDUCATIONAL AND USEFUL WORKS.

Price

7/6

THE BEST WORK FOR SELF-EDUCATORS.

THE UNIVERSAL INSTRUCTOR; or, Self-Culture for All.

A Complete Cyclopædia of Learning and Self-Education; meeting the Requirements of all Classes of Students, and forming a Perfect System of Intellectual Culture. With 2,000 Illustrations. In Three Vols., royal 8vo, each *7s. 6d.*; half-calf or half-morocco, *12s.*

"*The work is excellent, and it is to be hoped it may meet with the popularity it deserves.*"—ATHENÆUM.

6/-

THE DOCTOR AT HOME, AND NURSE'S GUIDE BOOK:

A Guide to the Structure and Composition of the Human Body; the Nature, Causes and Treatment of Disease; its Maintenance in Health and Strength, and the Prolongation of Life; with special Directions respecting the various Ailments and Disorders of Childhood and Womanhood. Edited by GEORGE BLACK, M.B. Edin., Author of "First Aid in Accident and Sudden Illness," &c. With Hundreds of Illustrations. Demy 8vo, cloth, 900 pages, *6s.*

"Doctors will be the first to testify to the value of such a work as this."—CITY PRESS.

5/-
or
3/6

"THE PRACTICAL MECHANIC SERIES" OF INDUS-

TRIAL HANDBOOKS. Profusely Illustrated. Demy 8vo, strongly bound in cloth, price *3s. 6d.* or *5s.* each.

1 The Stonemason and the Bricklayer. With Eleven Folding Plates and 224 Illustrations in the Text. *5s.*
2 The Domestic House Planner and the Sanitary Architect. With Sixteen Folding Plates and Sixty Illustrations in the Text. *5s.*
3 The General Machinist. With Four Folding Plates and Seventy-five Illustrations in the Text. *5s.*
4 The Building and Machine Draughtsman. With Eighteen Folding Plates and 155 Illustrations in the Text. *5s.*
5 The Carpenter and Joiner. With Twenty-five Folding Plates and 200 Illustrations in the Text. *5s.*
6 The Ornamental Draughtsman; Including Form and Colour. With Nineteen Folding Plates and Illusts. in the Text. *3s.6d.*
7 The Iron and Steel Maker. With Five Folding Plates and Thirty-two Illustrations in the Text. *5s.*
8 The Cabinet Maker. With Ten Folding Plates and Sixty-Two Illustrations in the Text. *3s. 6d.*
9 The Geometrical Draughtsman. With Seven Folding Plates and 126 Illustrations in the Text. *3s. 6d.*
10 The Student's Introduction to Mechanics. With 150 Illustrations. *5s.*

"The information has been supplied by men who are peculiarly well qualified to speak on the subject; and if our mechanics and artisans could be induced to master books of this kind, their interest in their daily work would be quickened, and, since skilled labour can always command the Market, their advancement in life would be secured."—THE LEEDS MERCURY.

5/-

A DICTIONARY OF THE TECHNICAL AND TRADE

TERMS of Architectural Design and Building Construction. Being Practical Descriptions, with Technical Details, of the Different Departments connected with the various Subjects; with derivations of, and French and German equivalents or synonyms for the various Terms. With Explanatory Diagrams. Demy 8vo, cloth, *5s.*

"The thoroughly explanatory character of the work gives it a high value, both as a book of reference, and as a practical guide for the young architect and builder. Technicality is shown to be no bar to a perfectly clear description of every term."—DAILY CHRONICLE.

WARD, LOCK & BOWDEN, Limited.

HIGH-CLASS BOOKS OF REFERENCE.

Price	
30/–	**A COMPLETE ENCYCLOPÆDIA FOR THIRTY SHILLINGS.** In Four Vols., royal 8vo, cloth, *30s.* ; strongly bound, half-Persian, *42s.* ; half-russia, *60s.* ; half-calf, *63s.* ; in Six Vols., cloth, *36s.* ; half-calf, *54s.*
36/– 42/–	**BEETON'S ILLUSTRATED ENCYCLOPÆDIA OF UNI- VERSAL INFORMATION.** Comprising GEOGRAPHY, HISTORY, BIOGRAPHY, CHRONOLOGY, ART, SCIENCE, LITERATURE, RELIGION AND PHILOSOPHY, and containing 4,000 Pages, 50,000 Articles, and Hundreds of Engravings and Coloured Maps. *" We know of no book* which in such small compass gives *so much information."*—THE SCOTSMAN. *" A perfect mine of information."*—LEEDS MERCURY.
18/–	BROUGHT DOWN TO THE AUTUMN OF 1892. **HAYDN'S DICTIONARY OF DATES.** Relating to all Ages and Nations ; for Universal Reference. Containing about 12,000 distinct Articles, and 130,000 Dates and Facts. TWENTIETH EDITION, Enlarged, Corrected and Revised by BENJAMIN VINCENT, Librarian of the Royal Institution of Great Britain. Medium 8vo, cloth, price *18s.* ; half-calf, *24s.* ; full or tree-calf, *31s. 6d.* *THE TIMES* on the 18th Edition :—" We see no reason to reverse or qualify the judgment we expressed upon a former edition, that the 'Dictionary of Dates 'is *the most Universal Book of Reference in a moderate compass that we know of in the English Lan- guage."*
7/6	**VINCENT'S DICTIONARY OF BIOGRAPHY,** Past and Present. Containing the Chief Events in the Lives of Eminent Persons of all Ages and Nations. By BENJAMIN VINCENT, Librarian of the Royal Institution of Great Britain, and Editor of "Haydn's Dictionary of Dates." In One Vol., medium 8vo, cloth, *7s. 6d.* ; half-calf, *12s.* ; full or tree-calf, *18s.* "It has the merit of condensing into the smallest possible compass *the leading events in the career of every man and woman of eminence.* . . . It is very carefully edited, and must evidently be the result of constant industry, combined with good judgment and taste."— THE TIMES.
7/6	**HAYDN'S DICTIONARY OF DOMESTIC MEDICINE.** By the late EDWIN LANKESTER, M.D., F.R.S., assisted by Distinguished Physicians and Surgeons. With an Appendix on Sick Nursing and Mothers' Management. With full pages of Engravings. In One Vol., medium 8vo, cloth gilt, *7s. 6d.* ; half-calf, *12s.* *" The best work of its kind."*—MEDICAL PRESS AND CIRCULAR *" The fullest and most reliable work of its kind."*—LIVER- POOL ALBION.
7/6	**HAYDN'S BIBLE DICTIONARY.** For the use of all Readers and Students of the Old and New Testaments, and of the Apocrypha. Edited by the late Rev. CHARLES BOUTELL, M.A. With many pages of Engravings, separately printed on tinted paper. In One Vol., medium 8vo, cloth gilt, *7s. 6d.* ; half-calf, *12s.* *" Marked by great care and accuracy, clearness com- bined with brevity, and a vast amount of information which will delight and benefit readers."*—THE WATCHMAN.

WARD, LOCK & BOWDEN, Limited.

HIGH-CLASS BOOKS OF REFERENCE.

Price 10/6 HOUSEHOLD MEDICINE: A Guide to Good Health, Long Life, and the Proper Treatment of all Diseases and Ailments. Edited by GEORGE BLACK, M.B. Edin. **Accurately Illustrated with 450 Engravings.** Royal 8vo, cloth gilt, price *10s. 6d. ;* half-calf, *16s.* "Considerable is the care which Dr. Black has bestowed upon his work on Household Medicine. He has gone carefully and ably into all the subjects that can be included in such a volume. . . . *The work is worthy of study and attention, and likely to produce real good."*— ATHENÆUM.

THE BOOK FOR AMATEURS IN CARPENTRY, &c.

7/6 EVERY MAN HIS OWN MECHANIC. Being a Complete Guide for Amateurs in HOUSEHOLD CARPENTRY AND JOINERY, ORNAMENTAL AND CONSTRUCTIONAL CARPENTRY AND JOINERY, and HOUSEHOLD BUILDING, ART AND PRACTICE. New, Revised and Enlarged Edition, with **about 900 Illustrations of Tools, Processes, Buildings, &c.** Demy 8vo, cloth gilt, price *7s. 6d. ;* half-calf, *12s.*

" There is a fund of solid information of every kind in the work before us, which entitles it to the proud distinction of being *a complete ' vade-mecum' of the subjects upon which it treats."*—THE DAILY TELEGRAPH.

7/6 BEETON'S DICTIONARY OF THE PHYSICAL SCIENCES ; Including Astronomy, Botany, Chemistry, Geology, Electricity, Sound, Light, Heat, &c. With **explanatory Engravings.** Royal 8vo, cloth gilt, *7s. 6d. ;* half-calf, *12s.*

7/6 BEETON'S DICTIONARY OF RELIGION, PHILOSOPHY, POLITICS, AND LAW. With **explanatory Woodcuts.** Royal 8vo, cloth gilt, *7s. 6d. ;* half-calf, *12s.*

7/6 BEETON'S DICTIONARY OF INDUSTRIES AND COMMERCE; Accounts, Agriculture, Building, Banking, Engineering, Mechanism, Mining, Manufactures, Seamanship and Shipping, Steam Engines, and many other Useful Articles. With **300 Explanatory Woodcuts.** Royal 8vo, cloth gilt, *7s. 6d.*

7/6 BEETON'S DICTIONARY OF LITERATURE, FINE ARTS AND AMUSEMENTS ; Architecture, Books, Heraldry, Journalism, Music, Painting, Sculpture, and many other Subjects pertaining to Culture and general Information. With **Explanatory Woodcuts.** Royal 8vo, cloth gilt, price *7s. 6d.*

The care and labour bestowed on these works have rendered them complete and trustworthy Encyclopædias on the subjects which they include. The latest discoveries, improvements, and changes have been noticed and duly chronicled in the various articles, and no pains have been spared to attain at once completeness, clearness, and accuracy in each book.

7/6 per Vol. THE INDUSTRIAL SELF-INSTRUCTOR in the leading branches of TECHNICAL SCIENCE and INDUSTRIAL ARTS and PROCESSES. With **Coloured Plates, and many Hundreds of Working Drawings, Designs, and Diagrams.** In Five Vols., demy 4to, cloth gilt, *7s. 6d.* each.

This work, devoted to the spread of Technical Education, appeals to all who take an interest in Manufactures and Construction, and in the progress and operation of practical Science. As a useful and-interesting book for youths and those engaged in self-education, it cannot fail to recommend itself, while it will be found a book of useful reference to the general reader.

" Promises to be *one of the most useful books ever issued* from the British press.' —FREEMAN'S JOURNAL.

WARD, LOCK & BOWDEN, Limited.

HELP FOR THOSE WHO HELP THEMSELVES.

Price	
6/-	*THE THIRD VOLUME OF THE SECOND SERIES OF* **AMATEUR WORK, ILLUSTRATED.** A Cyclopædia of Constructive and Decorative Art and Manual Labour. With Folding Supplements and Hundreds of Engravings in the Text. Crown 4to, cloth gilt, *6s.*
7/6	*THE SECOND VOLUME OF THE SECOND SERIES OF* **AMATEUR WORK, ILLUSTRATED.** With Folding Supplements and Hundreds of Engravings. Cr. 4to, cl. gilt, *7s. 6d.*
7/6	**MECHANICAL PASTIMES:** Volume 1. of the Second Series of "AMATEUR WORK, ILLUSTRATED." With Folding Supplements and Hundreds of Engravings. Crown 4to, cloth gilt, *7s. 6d.*
7/6	**THE AMATEUR MECHANIC.** Being the Seventh Volume of "AMATEUR WORK, ILLUSTRATED." With Folding Supplements, and about 1,000 Engravings. *7s. 6d.*
7/6	**THE AMATEUR'S STOREHOUSE.** Being the Sixth Volume of "AMATEUR WORK, ILLUSTRATED." With Folding Supplements and about 1,000 Engravings. *7s. 6d.*
7/6	**THE HOME WORKMAN.** Being the Fifth Volume of "AMATEUR WORK, ILLUSTRATED." With Folding Supplements and about 1,000 Engravings. *7s. 6d.*
7/6	**PRACTICAL MECHANICS.** Being the Fourth Volume of "AMATEUR WORK, ILLUSTRATED." With Folding Supplements and about 1,000 Engravings. *7s. 6d.*
7/6	**THE WORKSHOP AT HOME.** Being the Third Volume of "AMATEUR WORK, ILLUSTRATED." With Folding Supplements, and about 1,000 Engravings. *7s. 6d.*
7/6	**MECHANICS MADE EASY.** Being the Second Volume of "AMATEUR WORK, ILLUSTRATED." With Folding Supplements, and about 1,000 Engravings in the Text. *7s. 6d.*
7/6	**AMATEUR WORK, ILLUSTRATED.** Vol. I. With Folding Supplements and about 1,000 Engravings. *7s. 6d.*

Among the subjects treated of in these Volumes will be found:—Lathe Making — Electro Plating — Modelling in Clay—Organ Building—Clock Making—Photography—Boat Building—Book-binding—Gas Fitting—Tools and Furniture—Veneering—French Polishing—Wood Carving—Plaster Casting—Fret-Work—Decoration—Working Drawings—House Painting and Papering—Violin Making—Electric Bells—Brass Casting—Wood Jointing—Brazing and Soldering—Boot Mending and Making—China Painting—House Painting—House Papering—Gilding—Picture Frame Making—Printing—Pianoforte Tuning— Forge Work — Bird Stuffing and Preserving, &c. &c., with Thousands of Useful Hints.

Price	
15/- 18/- 21/-	**BEETON'S DICTIONARY OF UNIVERSAL INFORMA-TION:** SCIENCE, ART, LITERATURE, RELIGION AND PHILOSOPHY. Comprising about 2,000 pages, 4,000 columns, 25,000 complete Articles. In Two Vols., royal 8vo, with many Illustrations, *15s.;* half-Persian, *21s.;* in One Vol., half-roan, without Illustrations, *18s.* "*A most valuable work of reference.*"—THE TIMES.
15/- 18/- 21/-	**BEETON'S DICTIONARY OF UNIVERSAL INFORMA-TION,** relating to GEOGRAPHY, HISTORY, BIOGRAPHY, &c. With Maps In Two Vols., royal 8vo, cloth, with many Illustrations, *15s.;* half-Persian, *21s.:* in One Vol., half-roan, without Illustrations, *18s.* "*A combination of accuracy, compactness, compre-hensiveness and cheapness.*"—GLASGOW HERALD.

WARD, LOCK & BOWDEN, Limited.

STANDARD REFERENCE BOOKS.

Price	
10/6	*IMPORTANT WORK ON THE VIOLIN.*—SECOND EDITION. *Dedicated by Special Permission to H.R.H. the Duke of Edinburgh.* **VIOLIN-MAKING :** As it Was and as it Is. A Historical, Theoretical, and Practical Treatise on the Art, for the Use of all Violin Makers and Players, Amateur and Professional. Preceded by an Essay on the Violin and its Position as a Musical Instrument. By EDWARD HERON-ALLEN. With **Photographs, Folding Supplements** and 200 **Engravings.** Demy 8vo, cloth gilt, price *10s. 6d.* "A book which all who love to hear or play the instrument will receive with acclamation."—YORKSHIRE POST.
6/-	**EVERYBODY'S LAWYER (Beeton's Law Book).** Eighth and Entirely New Edition, completely Re-written and Re-composed. A Practical Compendium of the General Principles of English Jurisprudence. With copious Index. Crown 8vo, cloth gilt, *6s.* "The information is set forth in the clearest manner. . . . 'Everybody's Lawyer' may be trusted to prove most helpful."—THE DAILY CHRONICLE. "A volume which really contains a vast storehouse of useful legal lore."—THE LIVERPOOL DAILY POST. "We know of no work of its kind which is at once so simple, so clear, and so complete."—THE YORKSHIRE POST.
7/6	**BEETON'S DICTIONARY OF GEOGRAPHY :** A Universal Gazetteer. Illustrated by Maps—Ancient, Modern, and Biblical, and several Hundred **Engravings.** Containing upwards of 12,000 distinct and complete Articles. Post 8vo, cloth gilt, *7s. 6d.* ; half-calf, *10s. 6d.*
7/6	**BEETON'S DICTIONARY OF BIOGRAPHY.** Containing upwards of 10,000 Articles, profusely **Illustrated by Portraits.** Post 8vo, cloth gilt, *7s. 6d.* ; half-calf, *10s. 6d.*
7/6	**BEETON'S DICTIONARY OF NATURAL HISTORY.** Containing upwards of 2,000 Articles and 400 **Engravings.** Crown 8vo, cloth gilt, *7s. 6d.* ; half-calf, *10s. 6d.*
7/6	**BEETON'S BOOK OF HOME PETS :** How to Rear and Manage in Sickness and in Health. With many **Coloured Plates,** and upwards of 200 Woodcuts from designs principally by HARRISON WEIR. Post 8vo, half-bound, *7s. 6d.* ; half-calf, *10s. 6d.*
7/6	**A MILLION OF FACTS** of Correct Data and Elementary Information concerning the entire Circle of the Sciences, and on all subjects of Speculation and Practice. By Sir RICHARD PHILLIPS. Crown 8vo, cloth gilt, *7s. 6d.* ; half-calf, *10s. 6d.*
10/6	**THE SELF-AID CYCLOPÆDIA,** for Self-Taught Students. Comprising General Drawing ; Architectural, Mechanical, and Engineering Drawing ; Ornamental Drawing and Design ; Mechanics and Mechanism ; the Steam Engine. By ROBERT SCOTT BURN, F.S.A.E., &c. With upwards of 1,000 **Engravings.** Demy 8vo, half-bound, price *10s. 6d.*
12/-	**LAVATER'S ESSAYS ON PHYSIOGNOMY.** With Memoir of the Author. Illustrated with 400 Profiles. Royal 8vo, cloth, *12s.*
12/-	**BROOKES'** (R.) **GENERAL GAZETTEER ;** or, Geographical Dictionary. Medium 8vo, cloth, price *12s.*
7/-	**BROWN'S** (Rev. J.) **DICTIONARY OF THE BIBLE.** Medium 8vo, cloth, price *7s.*

WARD, LOCK & BOWDEN, Limited.

WARD & LOCK'S POPULAR DICTIONARIES.

Price	
	THE STANDARD **DICTIONARIES OF LANGUAGE.**
	THE CHEAPEST DERIVATIVE DICTIONARY PUBLISHED. *2s. 6d.*
2/6	The STANDARD ETYMOLOGICAL DICTIONARY of the ENGLISH LANGUAGE. By FRANCIS YOUNG. Large crown 8vo, cloth gilt, marbled edges, 500 pp., *2s. 6d.* ; half-russia, *5s.* ILLUSTRATED EDITION, cloth gilt, *3s. 6d.* ; half-roan, *5s.* "The work is brought well up to date. . . . *Altogether, for its size, it will be found to be the most complete popular Dictionary of our language yet published.*"—THE ATHENÆUM.
5/–	BREWER'S ETYMOLOGICAL & PRONOUNCING DICTIONARY OF DIFFICULT WORDS. By the Rev. E. COBHAM BREWER, LL.D. Large crown 8vo, 1,600 pp., cloth, *5s.*; half-roan, *6s.*
5/– 6/– 3/6	WEBSTER'S UNIVERSAL PRONOUNCING AND DEFINING DICTIONARY OF THE ENGLISH LANGUAGE. Condensed by C. A. GOODRICH, D.D. Royal 8vo, half-roan, *5s.*; ILLUSTRATED EDITION, cloth, *6s.* ; ditto gilt, *7s. 6d.*; half-morocco, *10s. 6d.*; SMALLER EDITION, demy 8vo, cloth, *3s. 6d.*
2/6 6/–	WEBSTER'S IMPROVED PRONOUNCING DICTIONARY OF THE ENGLISH LANGUAGE. Condensed and adapted by CHARLES ROBSON. Super-royal 16mo, cloth, *2s. 6d.* ; half-roan, *3s. 6d.* ; ILLUSTRATED EDITION, half-morocco, *6s.*
5/–	WALKER AND WEBSTER'S ENGLISH DICTIONARY. With Key by LONGMUIR. Demy 8vo, cloth, *5s.* ; half-roan, *6s.*
3/6	AINSWORTH'S LATIN DICTIONARY, English-Latin and Latin-English. Additions by J. DYMOCK, LL.D. Super-royal 16mo, cloth, *3s. 6d.*
3/6 2/–	NEW FRENCH-ENGLISH AND ENGLISH-FRENCH PRONOUNCING DICTIONARY. On the Basis of NUGENT. Super-royal 16mo, cloth, *3s. 6d.*; small fcap. 8vo, half-roan, *2s.*; New Edition, fcap. 8vo, wrapper, *1s.*; cloth, *1s. 6d.*
1/– 2/6	WARD AND LOCK'S NEW PRONOUNCING DICTIONARY of the ENGLISH LANGUAGE. Crown 8vo, cloth, 300 pp., price *1s.* ; Thicker Edition, half-roan, *2s. 6d.*
1/–	WEBSTER'S POCKET SHILLING DICTIONARY OF THE ENGLISH LANGUAGE. Condensed by CHARLES ROBSON. Imp. 32mo, cloth, 768 pp., *1s.*
1/– 2/–	WARD AND LOCK'S SHILLING GERMAN DICTIONARY. Containing German-English and English-German, Geographical Dictionary, &c. Crown 16mo, cloth, *1s.*; demy 32mo, half-roan, *2s.*
1/–	WALKER AND WEBSTER'S DICTIONARY. Containing upwards of 35,000 Words. Small fcap. 8vo, cloth, *1s.*; half-roan, *1s. 6d.*
6d.	WEBSTER'S SIXPENNY POCKET PRONOUNCING DICTIONARY OF THE ENGLISH LANGUAGE. Revised Edition. by W. G. WEBSTER, Son of Noah Webster. Demy 32mo, cloth, *6d.*
1d.	WEBSTER'S PENNY PRONOUNCING DICTIONARY. Containing over 10,000 words. Price *1d.* ; or linen wrapper, *2d.*

WARD, LOCK & BOWDEN, Limited.

Price	

THE
STANDARD GARDENING BOOKS.

10/6

ENLARGED AND REVISED EDITION.

BEETON'S NEW BOOK OF GARDEN MANAGEMENT.

A New and Greatly Enlarged Edition, entirely Remodelled and thoroughly Revised; forming a Compendium of the Theory and Practice of Horticulture, and a Complete Guide to Gardening in all its Branches. **Profusely Illustrated with Coloured Plates and 600 Engravings.** Royal 8vo, very handsomely bound, cloth gilt, bevelled boards, *10s. 6d.*

BEETON'S NEW BOOK OF GARDEN MANAGEMENT *is a complete and exhaustive work on the* THEORY *and* PRACTICE OF GARDENING *in all its Branches, embodying Full and Detailed Information on every subject that is directly or indirectly connected with the Art, leading up from the preparation of any description of Ground, to render it fit and suitable for Horticultural purposes, to the Culture of every kind of Flower Fruit, Vegetable, Herb and Tree that is or can be grown in it.*

"The work is exceedingly comprehensive . . . . *appears to leave no detail of the subject without adequate treatment."—* THE DAILY TELEGRAPH.

7/6

BEETON'S ILLUSTRATED GARDENING BOOK. A

Complete Guide to Gardening in all its Branches, and a reliable compendium of the Theory and Practice of Horticulture. **With Coloured Plates and Hundreds of Engravings.** Crown 8vo, cloth gilt, *7s. 6d.*

This work is of a most comprehensive character, showing how to Lay Out and Stock the Garden, and describing the Culture necessary for every Fruit, Flower and Vegetable that is grown in it. The work also treats exhaustively of Sites, Soils and Manures, Sequence of Crops, Garden Carpentry, Tools and Appliances, Greenhouses, Orchard Houses, &c.

6/-

BEETON'S BOOK OF GARDEN MANAGEMENT. The

Original Crown 8vo Edition. Embracing all kinds of information connected with Fruit, Flower, and Kitchen Garden Cultivation, Orchid Houses, &c. &c. Illustrated with a large number of **Engravings.** Crown 8vo, cloth gilt, price *6s.*; or in half-calf, *10s. 6d.*

3/6

BEETON'S DICTIONARY OF EVERY-DAY GARDENING.

Constituting a Popular Cyclopædia of the Theory and Practice of Horticulture. Illustrated with **Coloured Plates,** made after Original Water Colour Drawings, and **Woodcuts** in the Text. Crown 8vo, cloth gilt, price *3s. 6d.*

2/6

ALL ABOUT GARDENING. Being a Popular Dictionary of

Gardening, containing full and practical Instructions in the different Branches of Horticultural Science. With **Illustrations.** Crown 8vo. cloth gilt, price *2s. 6d.*

WARD, LOCK & BOWDEN, Limited.

GARDENING BOOKS.

Price	THE STANDARD GARDENING BOOKS—*continued.*
2/6	**THE GARDEN: Its Preparation and Arrangement.** Showing and Describing how Gardens are Laid Out ; the Tools and Appliances wanted for Garden Work ; the Structures with which Gardens are Furnished and Fquipped. **With many Illustrations.** Crown 8vo, cloth, *2s. 6d.*
2/6	**WORK IN GARDEN AND GREENHOUSE ALL THE** YEAR ROUND. Describing how Gardens are Kept, Stocked and Renewed ; Routine Work in Garden and Greenhouse all the year round ; the Training, Culture, and Propagation of Trees, Shrubs, Fruits, Flowers, and Vegetables. **With many Illustrations.** Crown 8vo, cloth, *2s. 6d.*
1/– 1/6	**BEETON'S GARDENING BOOK.** Containing full and practical Instructions concerning general Gardening Operations, the Flower Garden, the Fruit Garden, the Kitchen Garden, Pests of the Garden, with a Monthly Calendar of Work to be done in the Garden throughout the Year. **With Illustrations.** Post 8vo, cloth, price *1s. ;* or cloth gilt, with **Coloured Plates,** price *1s. 6d.*
1/–	**HOW TO MAKE A GARDEN.** Giving Complete Instructions on the Formation of a Garden. Describing every Operation that is necessary for the Conversion of a piece of Land into a well-arranged Garden. **With many Illustrations.** Crown 8vo, limp cloth, *1s.*
1/–	**AIDS TO GARDENING:** An Exhaustive and Reliable Summary of Articles of all kinds requisite for Garden Work in every branch. With clear and practical Instructions for the Construction, Heating and Ventilation of Glazed Appliances, Fixed and Movable. **With many Illustrations.** Crown 8vo, limp cloth, *1s.*
1/–	**THE GARDEN AND ITS WORK FOR EVERY MONTH** IN THE YEAR. Setting forth the best Modes and Means of Restoring worn-out Garden Ground ; the Renovation and Regeneration of Fruit Trees ; the Theory of Plant Life and Growth ; the Methods of Propagation ; the Management of all kinds of Fruit Trees ; and the Gardener's Out-door Work in every Season. **With many Illustrations.** Crown 8vo, limp cloth, *1s.*
1/–	**GREENHOUSE AND GARDEN.** A Complete Summary of the Treatment of Flowers, Fruits and Vegetables under Glass; Directions for Planting and Preserving Ornamental Shrubs and Trees ; the Culture of all kinds of Plants used as Food: Cultural Notes on all Varieties of Flowers ; and Instructions for Window Gardening and Management of Ferns. **With many Illustrations.** Crown 8vo, limp cloth, *1s.*
1/–	**KITCHEN AND FLOWER GARDENING FOR PLEASURE** AND PROFIT. A Practical Guide to the Cultivation of Vegetables, Fruits, and Flowers. With upwards of **100 Engravings.** Crown 8vo, limp cloth, *1s.*
1/–	**GLENNY'S ILLUSTRATED GARDEN ALMANAC AND** FLORISTS' DIRECTORY. Published Annually, with **Engravings** of the Year's New Fruits, Flowers, and Vegetables, List of Novelties, Special Tables for Gardeners, Wrinkles for Gardeners, Alphabetical Lists of Florists, &c. &c. Demy 8vo, price *1s.*
1*d.*	**BEETON'S PENNY GARDENING BOOK.** Price *1d. ;* post free, 1½*d.*

WARD, LOCK & BOWDEN, Limited.

Price	
	STANDARD NEEDLEWORK BOOKS.
7/6	**BEETON'S BOOK OF NEEDLEWORK.** Consisting of 670 Needlework Patterns, with full Descriptions and Instructions as to working them. Every Stitch Described and Engraved with the utmost accuracy, and the Quantity of Material requisite for each Pattern stated. Crown 8vo, cloth gilt, gilt edges, price *7s. 6d.*

SHILLING NEEDLEWORK BOOKS.

1/-

1 Tatting Patterns.	6 Guipure Patterns.
2 Embroidery Patterns.	7 Point Lace Book.
4 Knitting and Netting.	

NEEDLEWORK INSTRUCTION BOOKS

Imperial 16mo, ornamental wrapper, price *6d.* each.

6d.

1 Berlin Wool Instructions. With 18 Illustrations.
2 Embroidery Instructions. With 65 Illustrations.
3 Crochet Instructions. With 24 Illustrations.

SYLVIA'S NEEDLEWORK BOOKS.

Crown 8vo, fancy wrappers, profusely Illustrated, price *1s.* each.

1/-

1 The Child's Illustrated Fancy Work and Doll Book.
2 Sylvia's Lady's Illustrated Lace Book.
3 Sylvia's Book of Ornamental Needlework.
4 Sylvia's Illustrated Macramé Lace Book.
5 Sylvia's Art of Church Embroidery.
6 Sylvia's Book of Monograms, Initials, &c.
7 Sylvia's Illustrated Crochet Book.
8 Sylvia's Book of Drawn Linen Work.

10/6	**ART NEEDLEWORK.** With full Instructions. Demy 4to, cloth gilt, *10s. 6d.* With many Designs and Four Folding Supplements.
5/-	**THE LADY'S BAZAAR AND FANCY FAIR BOOK.** With 364 Illustrations. Crown 8vo, cloth gilt, gilt edges, price *5s.*
5/-	**LADY'S HANDBOOK OF FANCY NEEDLEWORK.** Uniform. Crown 8vo, cloth gilt, gilt edges, price *5s.*
1/- **6d.**	**THE KNITTER'S NOTE BOOK.** By E. M. C., Author of "The Lady's Knitting Book," &c. *1s.*; limp, *6d.*

BAZAAR AND FANCY-FAIR BOOKS.

Crown 8vo, fancy boards, price *1s.* each.

1/-

1 Sylvia's Book of Bazaars and Fancy-Fairs.
2 Sylvia's New Knitting, Netting, and Crochet Book.
3 Sylvia's Illustrated Embroidery Book.
4 Sylvia's Illustrated Book of Artistic Knicknacks.

WARD, LOCK & BOWDEN, Limited.

POPULAR SHILLING MANUALS.

WARD, LOCK, BOWDEN & CO.'S UNIVERSAL SERIES OF

SHILLING USEFUL BOOKS.

Price

1/-

1 Beeton's Shilling Cookery Book. With Cold. Plates.
2 Beeton's Shilling Gardening Book. Fully Illustrated.
3 Beeton's Complete Letter Writer, for Ladies and Gentlemen.
4 Webster's Pocket English Dictionary.
5 Beeton's Ready Reckoner.
6 Beeton's Pictorial Spelling Book.
7 Beeton's Family Washing Book. For Fifty-two Weeks.
9 Beeton's Investing Money with Safety and Profit.
13 Webster's Book-keeping. Single and Double Entry.
14 The People's Shilling Housekeeper.
15 Ward and Lock's Pocket English Dictionary.
16 Ward and Lock's English and German Dictionary.
18 Complete Etiquette for Ladies.
19 Complete Etiquette for Gentlemen.
20 Complete Etiquette for Families.
22 Etiquette of Modern Society.
23 Guide to the Stock Exchange and Money Market.
24 Tegg's Readiest Reckoner ever Invented.
25 The Bible Student's Handbook
26 The Complete Shilling Self-Instructor.
28 Speeches and Toasts : How to Make and Propose them.
29 Ward and Lock's New Pronouncing Dictionary.
30 Grammar Made Easy: The Child's Home Lesson Book.
31 Child's First Book of Natural History. Illustrated.
32 Webster's Dictionary of Quotations. With full Index.
33 The Pocket Map of London, and 32,000 Cab Fares.
34 Beeton's Recipe Book. Uniform with Beeton's Cookery.
36 Walker and Webster's English Dictionary.
37 Holiday Trips Round London. Profusely Illustrated.
38 The Holiday Companion, and Tourist's Guide.
39 Ward and Lock's Indestructible A B C. Illustrated.
39A Ward and Lock's Indestructible Alphabet.
40 Doubts, Difficulties, and Doctrines. GRANVILLE.
41 Beeton's Dictionary of Natural History. Illustrated.
42 The Dictionary of Every-day Difficulties.
43 Webster's Illustrated Spelling Book.

WARD, LOCK & BOWDEN, Limited.

POPULAR SHILLING MANUALS.

Price	
1/-	

WARD, LOCK & BOWDEN, Limited.

POPULAR SHILLING MANUALS.

WARD, LOCK & BOWDEN, Limited.

POPULAR USEFUL BOOKS.

Price	
	# THE LONG LIFE SERIES. Edited by GEORGE BLACK, M.B. Edin., Author of "First Aid in Accident and Sudden Illness," &c. Illustrated where necessary. Price *1s.* per Volume, neatly bound in cloth.
1/-	1 Long Life, and How to Reach It. 2 Eyesight, and How to Care for It. 3 The Throat and the Voice. 4 The Mouth and the Teeth. 5 The Skin in Health and Disease. 6 Brain Work and Overwork. 7 Sick Nursing. 8 The Young Wife's Advice Book. 9 Sleep: How to Obtain It. 10 Hearing, and How to Keep It. 11 Sea Air and Sea Bathing. 12 Health in Schools and Workshops. 13 The Human Body: Its Structure and Design. THE SATURDAY REVIEW says: *"It is not too much to say of them, as a series, that the shilling invested betimes in each of them may be the means of saving many a guinea."*
2/6	LONDON MEDICAL SPECIALISTS: A Classified List of Names and Addresses. Crown 8vo, cloth, *2s. 6d.*
1/-	## BEETON'S LEGAL HANDBOOKS. Crown 8vo, in strong cloth boards, price *1s.* each. 1 Property.—2 Women, Children, and Registration.—3 Divorce and Matrimonial Causes.—4 Wills, Executors, and Trustees.—5 Transactions in Trade, Securities, and Sureties.—6 Partnership and Joint-Stock Companies.—7 Landlord and Tenant, Lodgers, Rates and Taxes.—8 Masters, Apprentices, Servants, and Working Contracts.—9 Auctions, Valuations, Agency, Games and Wagers.—11 Conveyance, Travellers, and Innkeepers.—12 Powers, Agreements, Deeds and Arbitrations.—13 The County Court Handbook.—14 The Householder's Law Book.—15 The Licensing Laws.—16 The Married Women's Property Act, 1882.—17 The Bankruptcy Act, 1883.—18 The New Reform Act.
3/6	ORGAN BUILDING FOR AMATEURS. A Guide for Home Workers. Containing Specifications, Designs and full Instructions for Making every portion of the Instrument. By MARK WICKS. With upwards of 200 Illustrations. Crown 8vo, cloth gilt, *3s. 6d.* *"We have seldom met with a more clear, concise and exhaustive little treatise than this."*—MANCHESTER GUARDIAN.
3/6	FISHING TACKLE: Its Materials and Manufacture. By JOHN HARRINGTON KEENE, Author of "The Practical Fisherman," &c. With 254 Explanatory Diagrams. Crown 8vo, cloth gilt, *3s. 6d.* *"All anglers who are wise will find a niche for it in the sanctum.* It is a positive pleasure to recommend so unassuming and meritorious a book."—ATHENÆUM.
2/6	THE MAGIC LANTERN: Its Construction and Management. With 80 Engravings. Crown 8vo, cloth gilt, *2s. 6d.*

WARD, LOCK & BOWDEN, Limited.

www.ingramcontent.com/pod-product-compliance
Lightning Source LLC
Chambersburg PA
CBHW020852270326
41928CB00006B/660

* 9 7 8 3 7 4 4 7 8 9 6 6 0 *